"We're forever searching for moments of peace and feelings of happiness. And when we see glimpses of it, we're desperate for it all to stay with us as we go through the ups and downs of life. But as we know, peace and happiness don't always stick around. In *Stop Chasing Happy*, Phil helps us remember that lasting contentment and joy from God is what sustains us and stays with us. This book is a wise and comforting companion no matter what you're facing today."

Lysa TerKeurst,
#1 *New York Times* bestselling author and president of Proverbs 31 Ministries

"This book will speak deeply to your heart. In these days when so many are anxious and restless, Phil gives us a map to finding our true purpose in God—a life of meaning, hope, and joy."

Sheila Walsh,
author of *Holding On When You Want to Let Go*

"In *Stop Chasing Happy*, my friend Phil Waldrep reminds us that while happiness is fleeting, true joy can be found in living out your purpose. This book is a must-read for anyone who wants to discover the key to genuine satisfaction in life."

Dr. Robert Jeffress,
pastor, First Baptist Church, Dallas

"In today's society, happiness is often pursued as the ultimate goal in life. My friend Phil Waldrep shares stories of real people who lost themselves chasing the thrill of possessions and prominence and others who found true joy and contentment when they discovered their purpose in Christ."

Kirk Cameron,
actor and producer

"Discovering your purpose in life is made simple by Phil Waldrep's new book, *Stop Chasing Happy*. Rich in bibl⋯⋯⋯⋯⋯⋯⋯⋯al advice for finding the peace that comes ⋯⋯⋯⋯⋯⋯⋯⋯d."

cDowell,
Ministry

D1509586

"If you are ready to trade a performance-based mindset for confidence and satisfaction, then *Stop Chasing Happy* is the message you need. Writing with hope and understanding, Phil gives us a practical, Christ-centered guide to help us feel confident in our calling and experience real freedom and the power that comes from living life surrendered to God."

Alli Worthington,
author of *Standing Strong*

"We've seen firsthand this hard but hopeful truth: What happens to us matters far less than how we choose to respond to it. The deepest joy we all long for is available no matter our circumstances. Phil offers a fresh perspective on this truth for those seeking more than what the world has to offer."

Katherine and Jay Wolf,
authors of *Hope Heals* and *Suffer Strong*

"Phil Waldrep has the heart of a pastor, the mind of a teacher, and the ten-talent gift of a true storyteller, all of which serve him well as he shares the vital message of *Stop Chasing Happy.* Each chapter is filled with wisdom gleaned from 40 years of ministry, wrapped around the gospel truth found in the book of Philippians. His writing style is honest and straightforward without a wasted word, and whenever he points to our flawed human nature, Phil humbly admits his own challenges first. Both convicting and encouraging, *Stop Chasing Happy* is the perfect GPS to help believers find their way to genuine joy."

Liz Curtis Higgs,
bestselling author of *Bad Girls of the Bible*

"*Stop Chasing Happy* is a must-read for all who desire to follow hard after God. These pages flow out of the heart of Phil Waldrep—a faithful and dedicated servant of the Lord Jesus. Throughout the years, his walk has matched his talk as he has led thousands of men and women to find their place in the center of God's purpose for their lives. Everyone who reads this great book will be inspired to pursue God's priorities in a world searching for peace and happiness."

Don Wilton,
president of The Encouraging Word and
senior pastor of First Baptist Church, Spartanburg, SC

"Have you ever longed for a directing principle that would yield the peace and contentment for which you've been obsessively searching your entire adult life? Phil Waldrep has stepped up to the plate with your answer in his newest book, *Stop Chasing Happy*…and it's a grand slam!"

Andy Andrews,
New York Times bestselling author of
The Traveler's Gift and *The Noticer*

"I've known Phil and Debbie for more than a decade. Over the years I've watched them cheer on and lead men and women who are living out their God-given destiny. *Stop Chasing Happy* offers a fresh perspective for people confident in their calling or those just starting to discover who they were made to be. It's full of encouraging wisdom for living life with God's purpose at the center."

Candace Cameron Bure,
actress, producer, and *New York Times* bestselling author

"I wholeheartedly recommend *Stop Chasing Happy* to you. I know Phil Waldrep well, and he knows what he's talking about. In fact, I would call him an authority on the subject of joy! He has a lot of wise things to say about how to pursue God's purpose for your life. And having been around him for many years, I can assure you that you can trust that his words are not just opinions but are grounded on the truth of the Word of God. This book will bless you—and it might just radically change your life!"

Charles Billingsley,
Thomas Road Baptist Church, Liberty University

"My dear friend Phil Waldrep has written a book that reveals the secret to happiness. You will learn that happiness is not a goal you achieve, but rather a gift you receive when your focus is on the only One who can make you truly happy."

James Merritt,
lead pastor of Cross Pointe Church,
founder of Touching Lives Ministries

"The pursuit of happiness is something that can lead us all on a wild goose chase, only to leave us discontented, disappointed, and desperate for that next thing that promises to fill the void inside. My friend Phil lays out a wonderful roadmap showing us the way toward the true fulfillment that comes from knowing our God-given purpose."

Matthew West,
Grammy-nominated recording artist, songwriter,
author, and host of *The Matthew West Podcast*

"Happiness is seen by many in our culture as life's ultimate purpose. However, without finding your purpose in life, happiness will always be fleeting. *Stop Chasing Happy* points the way to discovering the joy that is much deeper than happiness."

Gary Chapman, PhD,
author of *The Five Love Languages*

stop

chasing

HAPPY

stop

chasing

HAPPY

PHIL WALDREP

HARVEST HOUSE PUBLISHERS
EUGENE, OREGON

The author is represented by The Christopher Ferebee Agency, www.christopherferebee.com.

For bulk, special sales, or ministry purchases, please call 1-800-547-8979. E-mail: Customerservice@hhpbooks.com

Cover by Faceout Studio, Amanda Hudson

Interior design by Angie Renich, Wildwood Digital Publishing

ᴍ is a federally registered trademark of the Hawkins Children's LLC. Harvest House Publishers, Inc., is the exclusive licensee of the trademark.

Stop Chasing Happy
Copyright © 2021 by Phil Waldrep
Published by Harvest House Publishers
Eugene, Oregon 97408
www.harvesthousepublishers.com

ISBN 978-0-7369-7879-8 (pbk.)
ISBN 978-0-7369-7880-4 (eBook)

Library of Congress Control Number: 2021935209

Printed in the United States of America

21 22 23 24 25 26 27 28 29 / BP / 10 9 8 7 6 5 4 3 2 1

For the staff of
Phil Waldrep Ministries

CONTENTS

CHAPTER 1

Better than HANDPPY

Rejoice in the Lord always;
again I will say, rejoice.
Philippians 4:4

I thought it was going to be another routine trip.

I left my office Wednesday afternoon, made two quick stops to get the laundry, and grabbed something for Debbie, my wife, and me to eat for dinner. When I arrived home, Debbie had everything packed for our trips the next day. I was flying to the Northeast to speak at the memorial service of a friend. Debbie was driving to Pigeon Forge, Tennessee, to start preparations for our Women of Joy conference that weekend. I would join her later in the week.

The next morning, Debbie drove me to the airport. After she stopped at the curb, I kissed her goodbye, grabbed my bag from the back seat, and headed to the security screening. Little did I know that in the next few days I was going to have four encounters that would change how I view life.

At the airport, I quickly passed through security and walked to my gate. I found a chair with some privacy and sat down. Moments later, the gate agent called my name. I hoped it was good news, and it was.

"Mr. Waldrep, thank you for your platinum status with our airline. I am pleased to tell you that you have been bumped up to first class," the agent said. She smiled and handed me my new seat assignment.

"Thank you! You just made my day," I said in response.

Any experienced traveler knows there is a distinct difference between a seat in coach class and one in first class. The seat in first class feels like a recliner. The flight attendants ask you every few minutes if they can get something for you. It is called first class for a reason.

And the people who sit in first class are different too. They tend to be wealthy because they have the money to buy an expensive ticket—or, like me, they travel extensively, rack up frequent flyer miles, and get promoted because of their status with the airline. Either way, first-class passengers rarely talk to each other.

After I boarded the plane, I casually put my carry-on bag away in the overhead and tucked the latest biography I was reading into the holder on the back of the seat in front of me. I looked at the other boarding passengers, wondering which one would sit by me.

Before long, a young woman who appeared to be no older than 21 sat by me. She was a beautiful, pleasant young lady, but she seemed out of place. In one sense, it would be odd for a young lady her age to have a position with a company that allowed her to travel frequently enough to get upgraded to first class. And in another sense, she didn't appear rich enough to buy the ticket. I confess that I stereotyped her as a daughter from a wealthy family.

She didn't acknowledge me. She sat down quietly and started staring at the floor. I respected her privacy, so I took out my book and started reading. Before long, the plane was airborne.

Several minutes into the flight, the flight attendant come through the cabin and asked if we would like some refreshments. I said, "Sure. I would like a diet soda." The young lady didn't speak. She only shook her head left to right, answering "no" with her body language.

A few minutes later, when I took a sip of my soda, I noticed the young lady was crying. It was then that I noticed her swollen eyes— swollen like those of someone in the morning after they had cried most of the night. This girl was hurting—and hurting deeply.

I didn't know what to say or if I should say anything. But my minister's heart discerns pain very quickly. And my pastoral nature wants to heal a hurting heart.

From past experiences, I know that an airplane can be a lonely place for a broken heart. For a brief second, my mind flashed to the tears on the cheek of a young chief petty officer in her Navy uniform who was escorting the body of her friend accidently killed in a military exercise. I remembered the sobs of a young man flying home to bury his mother after she contracted COVID-19 and died quickly thereafter. In every case that I could recall, a weeping person on an airplane was a grieving person.

So, I naturally concluded that this young lady was headed home because someone died. I wanted to help her process her grief by listening or offering a prayer for her and her family. I quickly prayed a silent prayer and asked the Lord for wisdom.

With as much kindness as I could muster, I said, "Ma'am, I don't mean to pry, but I noticed you are crying. I am a minister, and I'm also a dad—a dad with two daughters about your age. And, as a dad, I don't like to see young ladies cry. I am willing to listen if you want to talk."

"No, I'm fine," she replied with a hint of anger. Then she added, rather apologetically, "but thank you."

I simply smiled and turned my eyes to the pages of my book.

Then her voice broke the silence. She looked directly at me and said, "It's not fair!"

She wasn't screaming, but her voice was higher than the acceptable level for airplane conversations.

"It's not fair! I worked for this all my life. I earned it. The other girl must have slept with a judge or something because she didn't deserve it. And I'm not happy about it. In fact, I'm not happy, period! Do you understand?"

As I slowly glanced at the people around me, I noticed that

everyone was staring at me. They weren't sure what I said, but they were certain that I was the reason for this young woman being upset. Embarrassed, I immediately looked down and tried to appear that I was reading. Truth be told, I was feeling their stares. I started wondering when I could risk looking up again without seeing the agitation in the eyes of my fellow passengers.

Then, in a calm and lower voice, the young lady said, "Sir, I'm sorry. I shouldn't have responded that way. It's not your fault."

I looked at her, closed my book, and said, "You are right. I don't understand, but I sure would like to try to understand."

When I said those words, the young lady turned toward me with body language indicating that she was ready for a long conversation. "Well, my name's Jenna," she said as her right hand pulled the hair behind her ear.

"And I'm Phil," I replied.

With introductions behind us, Jenna began to share her story.

As a young girl, she struggled with a weight problem. All the girls in elementary school laughed and called her chubby. In junior high, none of the cool boys wanted to hang around her because they said that she was "too fat." Many nights she cried herself to sleep.

Although she never mentioned them, I assumed that her parents gave her love and support. It was the affirmation of her peers that she desired more than anything in the world.

Throwing her head back against the headrest, the tears slowly started flowing again. Then she continued. "I thought about becoming an athlete when I was in the ninth grade, but it didn't take me long to realize that wasn't for me. Then, I remember, on my six-teenth birthday, I made a vow to myself. I determined right then and there that I would become the prettiest girl in America!"

I thought about these words for a moment. It is a decision many people make. They think that they can prove their value by getting people to admit they are wrong about them. And if they succeed in convincing others, it will validate their worth. Then these people will feel good about themselves and be happy.

I didn't express my analysis to Jenna. I continued to listen to her story.

"So, I started watching what I ate. I started going with my dad to the gym, and his trainer helped me exercise. By the time I was 17, I was starting to feel good about myself." Her tears were no longer flowing. I sensed, at least for the moment, she was entering a pleas-ant time in her life's story. "But the girls still avoided me. Boys too," she said as she openly wondered why. "I started accepting myself, and I thought that would make me happy, but it didn't. I needed them to accept me."

Jenna proceeded to tell me that she thought the perfect way to get them to accept her was to prove beyond any doubt that she was as pretty as any girl in the world. And the best way to do that was to enter beauty pageants. But not just any beauty pageant. She wanted to enter contests that qualified her to be in the Miss Amer-ica pageant.

For the next four years, she took lessons on stage presenta-tion, how to answer questions, and the way to smile. A consultant helped her pick her clothes. Before long, she was winning qualifying contests to get into the coveted state titles that, in turn, would put her in the Miss America pageant.

But she kept winning only as the second or third runner-up. Never first place. And, for her, nothing but first place would do.

A little more than a week before we met on the plane, Jenna entered the final qualifying pageant for that year. She worked harder and prepared more than at any other time. She was certain she would win. But as the tears started flowing again, she told me she made the top ten. That was it. No first place, second or third runner-up. Just the top ten.

In her mind, that meant another girl was prettier, just like her friends said. Instead of validating her, the beauty pageants just confirmed her peers' cruelest words.

By now the wheels of the plane had touched the runway, and the pilot was starting to taxi to the gate. I knew our conversation was coming to a close.

"Well, Jenna, what are your plans now?"

My question was sincere, but I was hoping she would admit the futile efforts of trying to find value in the approval of others.

She smiled for the first time and said, "Well, I think I'm going to find a good-looking rich guy, get married, and have two wonderful kids. Yes, sir, that's what I'm going to do. And when I do," she continued as though she had found the answer to her problem, "I'm going to make sure all those kids who made fun of me in school hear about it. And the best part is," she said with a certainty that I had not heard in her voice, "I will finally be happy."

With those words, Jenna revealed her secret motivation. It wasn't to prove she was beautiful. It wasn't to hear the bullies say they were wrong.

She wanted to be happy.

I began to wish our flight was longer. I wanted to share with Jenna the true source of happiness, but the door was opening, and we had to exit the plane.

"Jenna, it's been great talking with you. I assure you that my wife, Debbie, and I will be praying for you to find that happiness," I said as we stepped off the plane.

The Happiest Woman I Know

The next morning, the forecast called for cold temperatures and some snow flurries. Being from the south, I'm not accustomed to these late spring blasts of cold weather, but New Englanders are. Dressed in my suit and a long wool overcoat, I drove to the small church that was the site of the memorial service. I greeted friends, and the funeral director gave me some instructions as we discussed the order of the service. There would be a song, another minister would briefly read some passages from the Bible, then another song, and then I would speak.

None of that was out of the ordinary. Memorial services are a part of what ministers do on a regular basis, both as a participant in the program and as a person in the congregation paying respect. Services tend to follow the same basic structure. But then the funeral director added something different, at least from my experience. He said, "The family requested that we have a microphone on the floor near the front and, after you finish your remarks, everyone who wishes may come and say a word about Marge."

Marge was the deceased, the wife of a pastor in New England. For years, she faithfully served alongside her husband in meeting the spiritual, emotional, and sometimes physical needs of their community.

Just a few days before her death, Debbie and I had flown to Vermont to visit her in the hospital as she fought her final battle with cancer. Instead of being sad, Marge had us laughing the whole time we visited. Laughter, I knew, was physically painful for her, but she didn't mind. She called it a "good kind of pain."

The nurses who came to her room often left with a tear in their eye. One said to us privately, "This is the happiest woman I know, and she is dying!"

That was Marge.

During the service, when the time came for me to speak, I tried to share words that would comfort the grieving family and friends seated in front of me. We laughed and cried as I recalled special moments from her life. And I reminded them of the hope that believers have in Jesus Christ. Then I announced that there was an open mic at the front if anyone would like to share a special memory.

One by one they came.

A single mom said, "I remember the time my baby was sick, but I had to go to work. I either had to stay home and go without pay or find someone to keep my sick child. Marge volunteered to come and stay."

One man, who seemed out of place for a funeral by the way he was dressed, shared how Marge would bring him food when she saw him on the street. He was a homeless man whom Marge befriended.

Still another lady told of Marge listening to her daily phone calls shortly after her mother died and the grieving daughter needed a sympathetic ear.

Standing behind the pulpit, I occasionally glanced at my watch. I had a plane to catch, and time to make the trip was slipping away. Nearly an hour passed as individual after individual told about the impact Marge had on their lives.

Finally, a little girl about 12 years old walked to the microphone. Tears flowed down her cheeks. You could see that she was poor, and I assumed didn't have the best family life. Choking back tears, she said, "Mrs. Marge was the best hugger in the whole world, and for some of us who don't get a lot of hugs, I will miss her."

I tried to keep my composure.

After the little girl sat down, no one else spoke. It seemed inappropriate after the words we just heard.

I closed the service with a prayer, expressed my love to the family members, and drove away. Planes don't wait even for memorial services to end.

As I settled into my seat on the plane, I found myself contrasting Jenna, the young lady on my flight earlier, and Marge. Marge never entered a beauty contest. She never wanted to. Being the center of attention was never her desire. She preferred hugs to applause, feeding the hungry instead of building a trophy case, and helping single moms with sick babies. And she had friends. Lots of friends. Friends who loved her for who she was and for the way she made them feel.

Jenna probably had just a few friends. The people around her, more than likely, were like her. They were people trying to prove their worth and were willing to use anyone or anything they could to do it. Yet, what she wanted was what my friend Marge possessed.

As I compared the lives of the two women, I couldn't figure out what Marge had that Jenna was missing. It was there, and it should have been obvious. But I needed to meet another person chasing happiness before everything came into focus.

Are You Happy?

As I exited the plane at the Hartsfield-Jackson Atlanta International Airport, I realized that I had a little over two hours until my next flight departed. I decided I would go to the airline lounge—an area in almost every terminal reserved for their frequent fliers to rest. I checked in at the desk, grabbed a snack, and went to find a place to sit. Most of the seats in the large, open area were taken.

Then I remembered that there was a small room in the back. I walked into it and, as I expected, there were plenty of seats. I found one in the corner.

As I sat down, I placed my snack on the small table beside me and reached into my travel bag to remove my Bible and a notebook. I wanted to write down a few thoughts for a sermon I was developing, and this was the perfect time and place to do it.

In a few moments, two other people entered the area. I didn't look up when they sat down. Like people flying in first class, people in airport lounges don't like to be disturbed. A few seconds later, however, I heard a deep, authoritative voice say, "Hey, are you a preacher?"

I instinctively knew he was talking to me.

I lifted my head and saw a gentleman standing with his arms folded, leaning against the doorway. He didn't appear to be the one who spoke, but I couldn't take my eyes off him.

Although he was in plain clothes, he had a police badge pinned to his shirt and a pistol strapped to his hip. Instead of speaking, he raised one finger to point at another man in the room, indicating where the question originated.

As I turned my head, I saw a beast of a man!

By beast I mean a man with biceps larger than my waist. His thighs looked like stone pillars on the front of a small-town community bank. Even his fingers had defined muscles!

When I made eye contact, he repeated his question. "Are you a preacher?"

"Yes, sir, I am," I said, hoping that he wouldn't beat me up for being one.

It was at that moment that I glanced down at the leather bag he was carrying. On the tag attached to it I saw the logo of a major professional wrestling group. I was looking at a real, live professional wrestler. Now I knew why he had muscles.

If this had occurred years earlier, I would have recognized him immediately. Like most young boys in the South, I watched professional wrestling earlier in my life. I stopped watching, however, when the language and the characters violated my moral conscience.

"What kind of preacher are you?" he asked. Before I could answer, he followed with another question: "Are you one of those preachers that believes God wants you to be wealthy and healthy?"

"No, sir. Not in the sense that I think you are asking," I said with an uncertain assurance in my voice.

I was starting to feel like we were facing off in the ring, and he was starting to taunt me as his opponent. The uncertainty in my voice made it appear that I feared getting smacked on the side of my head if I said the wrong words.

Then he leaned forward, looked me straight in the eyes, and asked, "Well, tell me. Are you happy?"

That was the first time anyone ever asked me that question.

"Yes, sir. I am," I said with a confidence that had not characterized my words before that point. And before I could think about it, I asked him, "Are you happy?"

"I'm trying to be," he answered with the lack of confidence in his words that characterized mine a few minutes earlier.

Then I asked what he meant by "trying to be." And like Jenna on my earlier flight, he started telling me his story.

He was born into a poor family. He didn't have the kind of toys or clothes other kids did. There were days, he said, when they didn't eat. But in high school he discovered weightlifting, and before long, his muscles made him the envy of the other boys. He joined the football team and became an outstanding athlete. But it was wrestling in high school where he excelled. Unlike the scripted professional matches, where the winner is determined in advance, high school wrestling was a matchup of strength and conditioning.

After high school, he went to work in construction and continued to lift weights to build his muscles—to "bulk up" as he called it. In the town where he lived, there was a promoter who staged wrestling matches. There were no television cameras or merchandise to buy. Just a ring with local wrestlers, all promoted by poorly printed signs at the local country store.

"I started going to these matches and decided to try it. I liked it, and I was good at it. Learned how to work the crowd," he said, as though I had never witnessed what he was describing. "Then, a larger promoter saw me. Asked me to join with him. He sent me to school to learn how to be a professional at it. Started paying me too," he said. "Before long, I quit my day job, and the rest is history."

"That's great, but it didn't answer my question," I responded, realizing that I was challenging a man who could crush me with one punch.

"And I said I was *trying* to be happy," he answered with a look that told me not to push the issue. "You see, I've got all the cars I want, including a Porsche and a Bentley. Got a nice house too. Lots bigger than yours, I bet," he said with a grin. Then he looked straight at me and said, "But someday I will have everything I want and everything I need, and then, I guess, I will be happy."

After he spoke those words, the police officer he hired to keep fans away in the airport said, "It's time to go."

He grabbed his bag and stood to his feet. I stood to mine. I reached out to shake hands.

"Do you mind if I ask your real name?" I knew enough about

professional wrestlers to know that their wrestling names rarely were their real names.

"Randy." He never offered his last name. He probably thought I could look it up on the Internet.

"Randy, I am going to pray that you find happiness. I doubt if you will find it in things. If you could, the happiest people in the world would be the richest," I said as we shook hands.

"Thank you, sir. I appreciate it." And with those words, Randy walked away.

I sat down and picked up my Bible. I started to make the notes that I originally had set out to do.

But I couldn't. I kept thinking about Randy. And then I started comparing his life to mine.

I didn't grow up in a wealthy family. My father was a welder, and my mother worked in a laundromat. We were an average, middle-class Southern family. I never went hungry as a child. My family was loving and supportive. The community around me and my extended family were supportive too. It never occurred to me when I was young that I was blessed, but I was.

Later, God gave me a wonderful wife and two precious daughters. Today, we have two godly sons-in-law and five precious grandchildren. I lead a wonderful ministry and work with a great staff. Together, we touch thousands of lives every year. Unlike the wrestler, I can walk through airports without anyone recognizing me. No one stops me for my autograph or a quick photo. I don't need an armed guard to get me to my next plane.

Life is good.

As I thought about the handshake with the wrestler, I remembered how he looked into my eyes when he said *thank you*. I couldn't read his mind, but I think, for a moment, Randy wanted to say that he wanted to trade places. For some strange reason, I felt I was the first person who crossed his path who told him they were happy. And for a brief moment, I think he was envious.

Randy didn't show his emotions like Jenna, but I think they were both seeking the same thing. They wanted to be happy and were willing to do or try whatever was necessary to get it. But they failed to see that chasing happiness is like seeking a pot of gold at the foot of a rainbow. You never find it because the base of the rainbow is always a little further on the horizon. The pot of gold doesn't exist. It's a myth.

I left my seat in the lounge and walked to my gate for my flight to Knoxville. On board, I started wondering, "Why am I different from Randy? I mean, things are nice to have, but why am I content with the basics?"

And I thought again about Jenna and my friend Marge.

Jenna and Marge. Randy and me. Two pairs of people who are totally different. But what is the difference?

I was about to find out.

Created for a Purpose

I arrived in Knoxville midafternoon, where I was met by one of our staff for the drive to Pigeon Forge, Tennessee. Pigeon Forge is a small resort town nestled in the foothills of the Great Smoky Mountains National Park. Along with its sister cities Sevierville and

Gatlinburg, it's one of the most popular destinations in the southeastern United States.

Because of the area's popularity, our ministry conducts several annual events in the city. One of the popular events we do is a three-day weekend conference called Women of Joy. At each conference, noted Christian musicians and popular speakers pour into the lives of thousands of women. And there is plenty of free time for fun and shopping too.

Friday afternoon, just before Debbie and I departed our hotel room for the opening session of Women of Joy, I received a phone call from a dear friend, Dr. Jay Wolf. Jay was the senior pastor of the First Baptist Church in Montgomery, Alabama. He asked me for a favor.

"Sure, what do you need?" I replied.

"My son, Jay, and his wife are coming through your hometown next week, and I was wondering if they could stop and visit. They are starting a ministry, and they need all the advice they can get," Jay said.

"I would love to meet with them. Tell them to call me, and we will set it up," I said.

Debbie and I were excited about meeting his son and daughter-in-law, Jay and Katherine Wolf. Our excitement wasn't limited to doing a favor for a friend, but we wanted to hear their story personally.

Sunday afternoon Jay, his son, called. We set Tuesday morning as the time for us to get together.

(Jay bore the same name as his dad but instead of using a middle name or a nickname, he used Jay as well.)

Jay and Katherine personified the American dream. Both came from successful families. They met while students at college, and after graduating, they headed to California. Katherine dreamed of being a model and, possibly, an actress. Jay wanted to be an attorney. Moving to California allowed both to pursue their dreams—Katherine in Hollywood and Jay at the Pepperdine Law School.

On April 21, 2008, Jay, who was completing his finals, decided to drop by their home during a break from the tests. He found Katherine on the floor in the kitchen. Something was seriously wrong.

At the hospital, doctors discovered Katherine experienced a massive brain stem stroke. The stroke resulted from a ruptured arteriovenous malformation—a rare congenital defect. Her chances of living were slim.

Fortunately, Katherine had a wonderful neurosurgeon who performed a risky operation, and her life was spared. Months of therapy eventually allowed Katherine to regain the ability to speak and, with the aid of a walker, to slowly walk.

Debbie and I sat listening to her story, hanging on every word. Jay sat quietly, letting Katherine tell her story. Finally, I leaned forward. "Katherine, I have one question," I said.

"Sure. Ask anything you like," Katherine replied, assuming I was going to ask a medical question.

"When you realized that your dream of being a model and actress was vanishing, how did you feel? I mean, you had to be sad and depressed. Right?"

Debbie gave me a look that implied my question might have crossed the boundary of what is proper to ask someone the first time you meet them. Looking back, however, I don't think I was asking for me. Subconsciously, I think I was asking for Jenna and Randy.

Katherine responded with a boldness and confidence you rarely find in a young person facing a lifetime of physical challenges.

"Not really," Katherine said. "I mean, I wasn't happy about it, but I've always believed I was created for a purpose. I originally thought it might be modeling or acting, but apparently God has a different purpose. The Lord is showing me what that purpose is, and I think it is to share my story to encourage people who are facing challenges in their own lives and to teach them about a God who loves them no matter what."

Jay added, "And we both believe that is our purpose now. It's going to be exciting to see how the Lord works."

But there was something different when they spoke. Theirs was a deep, confident joy that radiated from their faces. No sense of anxiety or bitterness. Just joy.

After we bid the Wolfs goodbye, I returned to my office and started making some notes in my journal. As I wrote her comment, the words gripped me. I read them again. This time I spoke them out loud.

"I've always believed I was created for a purpose..."

That was it. That was the difference between two beautiful young ladies pursuing careers as models. One had joy even when life didn't go as planned, and one felt that her world had come to an end when she didn't win.

And that Jay, whom many would advise to seek his own happiness by leaving his wife, could share the same goal and find joy in the process still amazes me.

Jenna and Randy were both chasing happiness. They thought it was just one pageant crown away or just a few more dollars in the bank. They were seeking something that they would never find.

> *You can find something*
> *better than happiness.*

Katherine Wolf taught me what my friend Marge knew. It was something Debbie and I knew but never could express in words. Fulfillment doesn't come from chasing happiness. Experiencing the best life has to offer doesn't come from having a perfect life with a perfect family living in a perfect environment. Joy comes from finding and doing what God created you to do, even when life is less than ideal.

Joy comes from finding your purpose.

It is discovering that everything about you—your talents, your personality, your appearance, even the time in history when you were born—was planned long ago by a God who loves you and invites you to be a part of His plan. And when you understand your purpose and pursue it, you find something that others rarely find. You find something better than happiness.

You find joy.

Truth to
REMEMBER

Your lack of joy comes from

your lack of purpose. Find

God's purpose for your life,

and you will find joy.

CHAPTER 2

Purpose Starts with
A MISSION

It is my prayer that your love may abound more and more, with knowledge and all discernment, so that you may approve what is excellent, and so be pure and blameless for the day of Christ, filled with the fruit of righteousness that comes through Jesus Christ, to the glory and praise of God.

Philippians 1:9-11

If you asked my family what was the one activity that I enjoy more than any other, they would say it was reading. And they would be right.

Since I was a small boy, reading has been my entertainment. But not just any book. My passion is biographies or autobiographies. I want stories about real people who made a difference. And the more pages a biography has, the more I like it.

I like reading biographies about the presidents of the United States, as well as about every major political figure in history. I like books about athletes, business leaders, and philosophers. But my favorite biographies are ones about ordinary people who didn't seek fame but impacted the world. Women like Rosa Parks and Mother Teresa. Or Corrie ten Boom, Anne Frank, and Florence Nightingale. And I marvel at the lives of men like George Washington Carver or Michael Faraday.

(Michael Faraday? He was one of the first people to understand electricity, and he created the modern electric grid. Albert Einstein considered him a genius, and Faraday's picture was one of only three portraits that hung in Einstein's office. Isaac Newton and James Clerk Maxwell were the other two.)

Whether I am reading a biography of a famous political leader or one of an ordinary person who impacted others, I am looking for one simple insight: What motivated them? What motivated them to endure criticism, hardship, and in some cases, imprisonment? What would prompt a person to risk their life, often losing it, to persist when others quit?

Without exception, people who impact those around them and the world in a positive way are people with a mission.

By mission I mean they have a goal to achieve something. They are trying to make the world a better place by feeding the hungry, caring for the suffering, or helping people achieve their dreams.

Mission is the reason behind their actions. It answers why they do something, not just what they do.

And this "why" motivates them.

Contrast that with people who are chasing happiness. They focus on the "what": things like a mansion in Palm Beach or heads turning in awe when they enter a room. But very few people who chase the "what" have biographies written about them. If someone writes one, they rarely hit the bestsellers list. People aren't interested in how much stuff someone has.

People admire individuals who know and live by their "why." Society admires these people because they have a reason for living and a compass to guide them through life. Coworkers admire them because setbacks don't destroy them. Peers admire them because they see the world as bigger than themselves.

But still, even people who live by their "why" never find joy. Yes, they have an inward satisfaction. Yes, they live without regrets...but deep, lasting joy evades them. To experience joy like few ever will, you must align your mission with God's mission. That is, His mission must become your mission too.

And when you understand God's mission for your life, and you make it your mission, you get all the benefits that others who live with a "why" have, but you get joy too!

The Mission to Magnify

Before you can understand your purpose, before you can experience unimaginable joy, you must start with understanding the mission your Heavenly Father has for you.

To begin, you need to understand the difference between your mission and your purpose. The mission is what God desires for you to accomplish. Your purpose is your assignment in accomplishing that mission.

To express it another way, your mission is why you do it. Your purpose is how you do it.

One of the most successful high school football coaches taught me the difference. Every day before practice, he looked at his players and said, "Everything we will do today is for one reason: to win the next football game."

And with the commanding voice of a Marine drill sergeant, he continued, "Every weight you will lift, every lap you will run, and every scrimmage you will play is designed only to win a football game. It is not to get a date with a cheerleader, or be cool on campus, or to get your name in the sports section of the newspaper. Everything, and I mean everything, we do is solely to win the next football game."

Often, he would add, "And because our goal is to win the next football game, we will avoid everything that keeps us from winning—things like not paying attention and not putting our all into everything we do." To make sure everyone got the point, he repeated the heart of what he wanted the players to hear again: "Remember, we have one objective: to win the next football game."

The coach taught me that when you have a mission, you can endure anything. Running until you think you can't put one foot in front of the other one. Sweating until you feel there isn't another drop of moisture in your body. Or walking into your home so sore you think you can't live another day. All that pain takes on meaning in the context of that next game. The thrill of winning—of accomplishing your mission—makes the hard stuff worthwhile.

Now, all Christians have the same mission. Our mission is to glorify God. That is why the Bible reminds us, "You are not your own, for you were bought with a price. So glorify God in your body" (1 Corinthians 6:19-20). And "whatever you do, do all to the glory of God" (1 Corinthians 10:31).

Glorifying God is a phrase often heard in church. Glorifying something means to magnify it. Do you remember when you were in a high school science class, and you took a smudge you could hardly see, put it on a small piece of glass, and slid it under a microscope? Looking into the lens, you saw particles that were invisible to your naked eye. The lens in the microscope magnified the image on the glass.

In the same way, our mission is to magnify God in our lives. Everything we do or don't do, and everything we say or refuse to say, should draw attention to who He is. In the Christian context, glorifying God means it is obvious to everyone around you that your relationship with Jesus Christ is the center and guiding force in your life. Glorifying God is your mission. It means that you obey His commands and follow the teachings of the Bible. It is trusting Him with your life.

But what about your purpose? Well, your purpose comes from finding your assignment—what God designed for your life.

Let's go back to the football illustration again.

Everyone on a football team doesn't do the same thing. There are two different groups of players on each team. Some players are offensive players. Their purpose is to advance the ball down the field and score. Others are defensive players. Their purpose is to prevent the other team from scoring. And even within these two groups are individual players with different assignments. All have a specific role to play.

Take the center and the quarterback, for example. The center's job is to snap the ball to the quarterback and to block the opposing players. The quarterback, however, must call the play, carry out the play, and make quick adjustments, like deciding where to throw the ball on a pass play. The center uses his size and strength to fulfill his purpose, while the quarterback uses his mind and quickness to fulfill his.

In the same sense, on the defensive side, a defensive tackle, a linebacker, and a safety all have different purposes. But a football team is more than the players on the field. There are coaches, managers, statisticians, trainers, and cheerleaders. They may not get the same recognition as the quarterback, but they, too, have an important role.

And what about the kid who isn't talented athletically? Does he have a purpose? Yes, he does! At the very least, his cheering in the stands affects the team spirit. One thing the COVID-19 crisis of 2020 proved was the vital role fans play in a game. Empty stadiums and arenas affected the intensity of the players on many teams. Ask any coach or player, and they will affirm that these empty seats affected their team's play.

So what did the players, coaches, cheerleaders, fans, and everyone else involved have in common? They all had the same mission: to win the football game. As believers, we all should have the same mission: to magnify God in our lives. But our assignment—our purpose—is different.

The Three Big Questions

It is easy for Christians to nod their heads and agree that their mission is to glorify God, but few see the connection between fulfilling that mission and a life filled with joy. So let's connect the dots by reviewing the three basic questions everyone asks: "Where did I come from?" "Why am I here?" "Where am I going when I die?"

Knowing you have a divine assignment will answer all of them.

Where Did I Come From?

Stonehenge is a prehistoric monument in Wiltshire, England. It is a ring of standing stones. Most of the stones are about 13 feet high and 7 feet wide, and they weigh about 25 tons. Researchers think they were placed in the ground around 3,000 years ago.

Everyone who visits Stonehenge, like all scientists who study the site, asks the same questions: *Where did they come from? Why are they here? What was their purpose?* It is hard to believe that, one day, a group of people decided to gather these large rocks and put them in a circle because they didn't have anything else to do. This back-breaking work took time and thought and planning. Scientists can only speculate the reasons for erecting these stones, but logic tells us Stonehenge's builders had a purpose.

In the same way, every human wonders where we came from. Are we the result of cosmic forces that produced human beings? Or did God create us?

Why Am I Here?

Most people think the purpose of life is to have a good time, to get all you can while you can, and to have a party. Success is the goal. In other words, chase happiness.

But if it works, why are most people unhappy?

Even Christians fall for this. Most of us want to do something "big" for God. We may think the only divine assignments our Lord gives are major ones in the public eye. We may try to mask our selfish desires by saying God has called us to achieve certain goals. We try to align God's plans with our plans rather than aligning our plans with His. If we are in a ministry, we want to be a prophet like Jeremiah or a preacher like Billy Graham. We want great crowds to come hear us like they did for John the Baptist in the New Testament. If we own a business, we want to be successful so we can give lots of money to the work of God. Or if we are employed, we want to be promoted or acknowledged as employee of the year so we will have a broader platform to influence people.

The motive behind these goals may appear to be pure, but they are driven by a need for recognition and approval. That is why many Christians lack joy in their lives. They think that they are here to be successful. They naively think that joy comes from doing big things for God.

Granted, you should desire to be the best you can be. Success is not a sin, but success is not fulfilling. Finding and doing God's purpose for you is. If it is highly visible, wonderful! But if God has a different purpose for you, visibility will never bring you joy.

> *Success is not a sin, but success is not fulfilling.*

Several years ago, when I spoke at a church in Tennessee, I met an elderly lady named Sue. Sue had the joy of the Lord! She kept telling me how much she loved the ministry she had, and how honored she was that God assigned her to do it.

When I asked about her ministry, I expected to hear about a large organization that was impacting thousands. Instead, I heard about a ministry that wasn't the envy of most. Sue told me that for 45 years she has cared for a mentally and physically challenged brother. "Oh," she said, "I work at a job here in town to earn money to pay the bills, but my calling is to glorify God by taking care of my brother, and that gives me joy."

Joy? Caring for a physically and mentally challenged brother brings you *joy?* I didn't verbally express those words, but the thought went through my mind.

When I thought about her remark later that day, I realized why I couldn't understand her joy. I was open to the Lord's assignment for my life if it corresponded with my plans and brought the desired results I craved. But the fulfillment and joy we seek is only found when we align our desires and our plans with His. Life isn't about making God fit into our plans. It's about us fitting into His.

What Happens When I Die?

Jesus told a story in Matthew 25 about a man who went away for a long time. He needed three of his servants to invest his money while he was gone.

He knew every servant's ability and limitations. Based on that, he gave one servant five talents, another three talents, and one a single talent. (A talent was a unit of money.)

The first two did as they were told and invested the money. The third one didn't. He hid the one talent the man gave him. Maybe he thought his assignment didn't matter. After all, it didn't appear to be significant. Or perhaps he thought the owner would never return and, if he did, he wouldn't care.

But when the man returned, the first two were applauded and recognized for their faithfulness. The third was rebuked.

In this story, the man represents our Heavenly Father who has given us a purpose for living. He assigned us a responsibility and expects us to do it. When we do it, we make the impact that He intends, and God multiplies our efforts many times over to advance His kingdom.

As a believer, one day you will step into the presence of your Heavenly Father. He won't care how wealthy or famous you became. God only cares if you put your trust in His Son for salvation and if you fulfilled what He wanted you to do. If you did, you will hear the words the man spoke to the obedient servants: "Well done, good and faithful servant."

Taking Off the Pressure

If God's plan for me is to magnify Him with my life, then there are a few truths that will relieve the pressure of trying to be happy.

I Was Created for a Purpose

Science sees human beings as the result of a biological act that occurred when a sperm from a male and an egg from a female united. It may have been planned, or maybe it wasn't. It can occur through natural means or in a petri dish. To unbelieving scientists, the creation of human life is a roll of the dice with different DNA factors fighting for dominance.

From God's perspective, nothing could be further from the truth. Your conception was a divine act with the God of the universe involved in every minute detail. The psalmist, realizing this truth, expressed his thanksgiving to God when he wrote, "I praise you for I am fearfully and wonderfully made" (Psalm 139:14).

In the Old Testament, God appointed Jeremiah to the role of a prophet. Jeremiah's mission was to warn Israel of the dangers of forgetting God and failing to serve the Lord. When Jeremiah wrote about discovering his purpose, God revealed to Jeremiah how He was involved in the prophet's formation before the man was born. Quoting the Lord, Jeremiah wrote, "Before I formed you in the womb I knew you, and before you were born I consecrated you; I appointed you a prophet to the nations" (Jeremiah 1:5).

When you were created in your mother's womb, your Heavenly Father oversaw every detail to make sure you had everything you needed to fulfill His plan for you.

But it didn't stop there. God even chose when and where we would be born. When I reflect on my life, I know that I couldn't do what God called me to do if I lived in the 1600s or in North Korea. The people born then and there had or have the same mission (to glorify God), but their assignment was or is different from mine.

Jeremiah had a highly visible assignment. His assignment, however, wasn't more important than the assignment God has for you. Jeremiah spoke to a nation. Your assignment might be ministering on a regular basis to one person. But considering how every person is valuable in the sight of God, then your assignment—highly visible or less visible—is equally important in God's plan. When you find your purpose, you will say, "I was made for this!"

I Have a Compass to Set My Priorities

If God created you for a reason, and you dedicate yourself to it, it becomes clear what you should and should not do with your life.

You should prioritize your personal relationship with Christ.

You should see hurting people and share their struggles.

You should value your relationships with your spouse, children, family, and friends.

You should control your schedule and prevent your work from destroying relationships.

You should build healthy boundaries for your physical, emotional, and spiritual well-being.

Allowing your mission to set your priorities, you now have time to do the things you should and the courage to say no to the things you should not.

I Have a Guide to Help Me Make Decisions

If God is the originator of your purpose, and your mission is to draw attention to Him, then His Word, the Bible, becomes your guide when making decisions. God's Word points out the sin you must avoid, tells you the truth you must follow, and helps you understand how the Holy Spirit empowers you to do both.

Recently, I was traveling to speak in a small, rural church in Mississippi. I had no idea how to get there. All I had was an address. Before I left home, I programmed the address in the navigational app in my vehicle. As I drove out of my neighborhood, a voice and a visual map told me every turn to make. Occasionally, the voice didn't speak for miles. But I was going in the right direction and following previous instructions. Even if I got distracted and missed a turn, the moment the app realized my error, it told me how to get back on the right road.

The Bible is your map. It tells you where your Heavenly Father wants you to go and tells you how to be what He desires. The Holy Spirit is the voice that speaks to your heart, helping you make decisions and apply what the Bible tells you.

Personal Application

It's tempting to jump to the details of having joy before you determine your mission and accept your purpose. If your motivation is right, your purpose will be clear, and you will be able to overcome the challenges to your joy. But trying to find a shortcut or trying to pick and choose what you want only results in frustration and a greater lack of joy.

To begin your journey to joy, write a personal mission statement for your life. Summarize your "why" in a single sentence. Try to avoid including any activity that might be taken away (job, hobbies, teaching a Bible class). They express your "what" more than your "why."

Here is my personal mission statement: *I will glorify God by being a follower of Jesus Christ, being a godly husband, father, and grandfather, and by making an eternal difference in the lives of people.* Notice that I didn't mention my ministry or my speaking. That is *what* I do to fulfill my life's mission statement. But if the day comes when I can't speak or lead a ministry, I can continue living my mission statement.

Your mission statement isn't a profound or technical statement. It is simply your "why," and it becomes your standard for living.

Write your mission statement on a sticky note and put it on the front cover of this book as you start the journey to help you find your assignment in God's plan.

Truth to REMEMBER

Your mission gives you a purpose. Your purpose gives you significance. Your significance gives you fulfillment. And fulfillment gives you joy.

CHAPTER 3

Purpose Reveals Your
POTENTIAL

I am sure of this, that he who began
a good work in you will bring it to
completion at the day of Jesus Christ.

Philippians 1:6

Several years ago, I started reviewing the great leaders of the world. I wanted to find one who—better than the rest—understood the mission God gave them to glorify Him, and to see how they discovered their purpose in that mission.

I had a few prerequisites. I wanted someone who had a clear understanding of glorifying God. I wanted someone who faced difficult choices when the "why" was challenged. And I wanted someone who paid a heavy price for staying the course. I wanted someone who wrote about their feelings when they were going through those experiences. I wanted to know how they felt and what advice they would give to others.

The person who fit all my prerequisites was the apostle Paul.

Next to Jesus, Paul probably is the best-known personality in the Bible. He wrote most of the books in the New Testament. Yet, many people aren't aware of how Paul moved from chasing happiness to living with joy by having the right mission and purpose.

Paul was born in Tarsus, a city at the mouth of the Berdan River in modern-day Turkey. His birth name was Saul. His parents were Jewish, and, like most Jewish families, ancestry was very important. They could trace their roots back to the tribe of Benjamin. Little is known about his parents except that his father was a practicing Pharisee and a Roman citizen. No one knows how or why his father became a citizen of Rome, but it gave him certain rights that many of the Jews did not have. That citizenship passed to Saul.

As a young Jewish boy, two things were expected of Saul: to develop a marketable skill and to learn the Old Testament. Saul learned to make tents from the hides of goats. And, when he was about 13 years old, he went to Jerusalem to study under an effective Jewish teacher named Gamaliel.

Saul became passionate about stopping the spread of Christianity. He saw followers of Christ as people who were dishonoring God. He was so passionate about it that he devoted his life to finding ways to arrest or kill Christians. When Saul was about 30 years old, he witnessed the stoning death of Stephen, one of the early church's most vocal witnesses to the claims of Jesus. The brutal, painful death of Stephen did not upset Saul. Instead, it emboldened him.

Saul spent the next few years devoting his life to harassing, persecuting, and killing believers. And he made a name for himself doing it. He not only disrupted Christians' meetings, but Saul went into their homes to hurt them. When Christians heard that he was coming to town, fear often gripped their lives.

Saul was on a mission, but it was the wrong mission. You can have a consuming drive to achieve a goal, but if the mission is wrong, your purpose will be wrong, and it will never result in joy. Saul's actions were selfish. He became a Pharisee, and Pharisees loved the admiration of others. He wanted people to admire him. His motivation was for the wrong reasons.

Once Saul started getting recognition from influential people, he went to the Jewish religious leaders and requested permission to go to Syria to arrest professing Christians. But on a trip to the city of Damascus, he experienced something dramatic. God spoke verbally to Saul and made clear to him who Jesus was. Immediately, Saul became a believer in Jesus Christ. And as a result, Saul changed his name to Paul.

The Bible never explains the name change. In the Old Testament, God changed the names of some personalities after He gave them a new direction in life. People like Abram and Sarai had their names changed to Abraham and Sarah. And Jacob became Israel.

It is possible some of his fellow believers shared with Paul how Jesus changed the name of one of His disciples, Simon, to Peter.

Perhaps, Paul wanted a new name to denote the change in his life. Or, maybe, Paul started using his new name to broaden his appeal to a non-Jewish audience. Paul was a Greek name, while Saul was a Jewish one. Whatever the reason, Paul was a different person.

As a new Christian, Paul spent several years listening and learning. He helped church leaders when they needed help. And along the way, he became a church leader too.

During these times, Paul grasped the source of lasting, fulfilling joy. It was to glorify God in everything he did and everything he was. He expressed his life's mission statement in Philippians 1:20: "It is my eager expectation and hope that I will not be at all ashamed, but that with full courage now as always Christ will be honored in my body, whether by life or by death." Understanding his mission, Paul was ready for God to reveal his role in God's plan, his purpose for living.

Seeing the need to spread the message of Christ, the Christians at Antioch appointed Paul and another church leader, Barnabas, to become missionaries. As missionaries, Paul and Barnabas stayed in one place long enough to share the gospel, teach new believers, and establish a church. Later, Paul teamed with another church leader named Silas. In all, Paul would spend the rest of his life preaching, teaching, and mentoring believers.

It was during these missionary adventures that Paul saw the need of writing to the churches he'd helped start. Some of them had questions, and some needed encouragement. Many of these letters—inspired by the Holy Spirit—are part of the New Testament today.

You might think Paul had a life filled with excitement and rarely had problems. But these years were hard. Civic authorities and Jewish leaders conspired to kill Paul, just as he had done before he discovered his purpose. He often was beaten and left for dead. He spent weeks in nasty jails because of the impact that he was making. Paul often was emotionally drained. He never accumulated much money, and he was often dependent on churches to provide for his basic needs. Yet, through it all, Paul maintained a joy that was the envy of everyone around him.

It is hard for us to imagine Paul having joy when life was difficult. It is easy to understand it when everything is exciting. But how could Paul or anyone have joy when things are rough?

Paul's secret to deep, fulfilling joy was settling what his mission in life was and willingly accepting God's assignment—Paul's purpose for being born.

Paul didn't write an autobiography like people in the modern age. But he came close. He wrote a letter to a church he helped start—the church at Philippi. Today it is included in the Bible as the book of Philippians. In this letter, Paul gives details about his life's journey and how he stopped chasing happy and started pursuing his purpose.

How could anyone have joy when things are rough?

If Only I Could Be Someone Else...

Several years ago, a church in a large city invited me to speak in their Sunday morning services. I arrived Saturday afternoon at the hotel, parked my car, and went into the lobby to register.

As soon as I stepped through the doorway, I experienced the shock of my life. Standing in the lobby were over 50 Elvis impersonators! I discovered I was staying at the host hotel for an Elvis Presley impersonator convention.

After I checked into my room, I returned to the lobby to get a soda. I couldn't resist the temptation to sit down for a few minutes and observe. Here were young men and old men, tall men and short men, and even a few women. All trying to be the best Elvis in the world.

Later, I stood outside the ballroom and watched the competition. I noticed most were good singers and dancers. The best ones had a good stage presentation. No doubt they all could have a successful music career if they tried. But every person on the stage was trying to be Elvis Presley. It seemed that none of them were happy being themselves, especially when performing.

A common attribute of unfulfilled people is believing they would be happy if they could be someone else. They are easy to spot. Just listen to their conversations. They include a lot of sentences with *if*:

> "Well, I would have a lot of friends if I had her personality."

> "If I could get a better job, my life would take a turn for the better."

"If I was as attractive as she is, I would have the husband of my dreams too."

If only… How would you complete the sentence?

If always is linked to happiness. *If* never is linked to joy. Joy is being who you are. It is being what God wants you to be. It is doing what God created you to do.

What you believe about yourself affects how you feel about yourself. If you focus your attention on what people want you to be, you become fake and inauthentic. You act solely to please them. Before long, you are one thing to one person, while being something different to another.

Living to get the approval and acceptance of others destroys joy. With your joy gone, you emotionally hide. You worry that if people meet the "real" you, they will reject you. Insecurity grows. You start avoiding particular people or places. Life becomes a series of actions to avoid people discovering who you really are. Or you go to the other extreme. You try to control every person or situation by appearing strong. Arrogance becomes your biggest trait. But insecurity and arrogance keep joy away. Or you might feel so insecure and worthless that you allow people—even your family members— to control your life, even abusing you.

When Paul wrote to the church at Philippi, he didn't begin his letter with a list of things to do to have joy. Instead, he started by reminding believers of the foundation of their joy; that is, what they must understand to attain something deeper than happiness.

Remember Who You Are

In the fall of 2016, Netflix released a new series called *The Crown*. It is a historical drama about Queen Elizabeth II. The series begins with her marriage to Philip, Duke of Edinburgh, and continues to the modern day.

For many Americans, royalty is just a title with lots of pageantry. The series, however, reveals that a reigning monarch has responsibilities and a code of conduct because of their position. The king or queen must never forget who they are.

Neither should you.

Before Paul discussed joy, he reminded the Philippians in his opening remarks who they were. He called them "saints in Christ Jesus" (Philippians 1:1). You may think of a saint as an individual who, because of their good deeds, was honorable above others. In fact, some churches classify a specific set of individuals who lived unselfishly as saints. But according to the New Testament, every Christian qualifies as a saint. No one person in the Bible is called a saint. Instead, the word *saints* is always used to describe a group of people.

If you know Jesus Christ personally, you are a saint. Not because of what you did, but because of what He did. His death and resurrection opened the door for your redemption. And through your relationship with Christ, you, like all believers, are a saint.

As a saint, you are special in God's eyes. It means you are set apart. As Max Lucado said, "If God had a refrigerator, your picture would be on it." And the word *saint*, in the original Greek that Paul used, means you are set apart for a purpose.

*Through your relationship with Christ,
you, like all believers, are a saint.*

Remember What You Have

People who chase happiness think they are missing something. They feel they will be happy when they add one more thing to their lives, like a spouse, a child, money, or prestige. But when they get it, happiness eludes them.

When I was a teenager, I wanted a car. I thought it would make me the most popular boy at school. And, in my mind, being popular would make me happy.

I got the car but not the popularity. Before long, I was thinking the problem was the car. I needed a different kind of car. Finally, I traded my car, but nothing changed. Emotionally, I was the same.

My father helped me come to grips with the situation. He reminded me that I was one of the few students at my school who had a car of any model. Most of the students at my school came from families that struggled to buy the basics of food and shelter. Instead of complaining, I should remember what I had and be grateful.

You will never experience joy if you stay focused on what you don't have rather than on what you have. And it's not just material things. It's also what you have in your spiritual life.

When Paul greeted the Philippians, he prayed that they would experience grace and peace—two things they experienced when they met Christ, and two things Paul wanted them to continue to experience. Grace occurs when God gives you what you do not deserve. It is a gift. You can't earn it; you just receive it. Grace gave you salvation. And that should make you grateful.

And what's the result of grace? Peace. Peace means all is well. No worry, anxiety, or sleepless nights. Now, Paul didn't randomly use these two words. He put them in a specific order. Grace always precedes peace. In all of Paul's letters in the New Testament, he opened with a greeting for the readers, and grace appears before peace every time.

Until you know and live by grace, you will never know the peace that leads to joy.

Remember Who You Have

God didn't create us to be isolated from people. Nor did He intend for people to be the source of our joy. Too many believers try to find their fulfillment in their marriages, their children, or their grandchildren. Others find it in a close friend. But take the people away, and they aren't happy.

People can add to our joy, but they are not the source of our joy. The source of joy is Jesus. That is why Paul said that grace and peace came "from God our Father and the Lord Jesus Christ" (Philippians 1:2).

Your relationship with Jesus is the only place where purpose is found. Without it, you will never find joy. With it, you are free to experience everything God has for you to enjoy.

It is a liberating thought. Regardless of how people treat you, your joy can remain. People can't give it, and people can't take it away.

Go Back to the Beginning

When a person is chasing happiness, their attention stays on the present. Their focus is on what they are feeling at any given moment. Their attention is on what they presently lack.

Purpose gives you a broader perspective. It looks back to where you were, honestly evaluates the present, and stays focused on the future.

In the opening remarks in Philippians, Paul took the believers back to the start of their Christian life. He reminded them of their partnership with him "in the gospel from the first day" (verse 5). Sometimes you need to stop what you are doing, sit down, and see how far you have come in your life. Can you recall your emotions and anxiety before you became a Christian? Do you remember how things you thought would bring you happiness didn't? And can you recall the days after coming to Christ when you experienced a deeper meaning in life?

These memories are important. Think of your salvation experience like an anchor. An anchor, when lowered, keeps a ship from drifting. In calm seas, a ship can drift slowly, taking it far from where it needs to be. In a storm, if the anchor is bedded in the right place and in the right way, the storm can't move the ship or damage it. When your life is anchored in Christ, it prevents a crisis from putting your life in chaos. It gives you stability.

Honestly Evaluate the Present

People who remember and learn from the past can evaluate the present effectively. Those who don't remember are controlled by their present circumstances and emotions. That is why Paul recalled his relationship with the Philippians from the "first day unto now" (verse 5). Joy in the present often comes by remembering where you have been and how your Heavenly Father worked in the past.

Shortly after Debbie and I married, our nation went through a financial recession. It affected our income and our ministry. Churches and people who supported us in the past were unable to give. At night, all my mind could see were the bills to be paid and how little money was in the checking account. I was fixated on the present, and it robbed my joy. I couldn't see any hope for the future.

During that time, I visited an elderly relative. We sat on the front porch of her old home and talked about the present crisis. But laughter characterized her life, and she wasn't concerned.

She grew up in the rural south. Her family was poor, growing the food they ate. Their only income was the cotton they grew and sold.

I asked, "How can you have joy in the middle of this financial crisis?"

"Son, I don't think about today. I think about yesterday," she said with a smile. "I remember the Great Depression of the 1930s. We literally didn't have food for days." She leaned toward me and added, "But we both ate something this morning, didn't we? I remember when our family almost lost our little farm. Couldn't pay the taxes on the land." She paused, and a tear ran down her cheek. "But God provided. One of our neighbors told Papa that the Lord blessed him a few years back with a good crop, and he put some money back and promised the Lord that he would use it when a friend had a need. The man paid the taxes and told Papa all he wanted in return was a ham when he killed hogs that fall," she added.

Then she looked at me and said, "Son, it is bad. But it could be worse. And if the Lord brought us through then, He will bring us through now."

Perspective changes everything. Remembering the faithfulness of God in the past gives joy in the present.

Before I left, she told me that her father quoted a particular verse every night to his family during the hardest times. And she said that she read it every night still. She opened her worn Bible—an old King James version that she had had for years. There, circled with a red pencil, was Psalm 30:5. She read it to me: "For his anger endureth but a moment; in his favour is life: weeping may endure for a night, but joy cometh in the morning."

I keep that verse marked in my Bible too. It challenges me to honestly evaluate my present circumstances by the past faithfulness of God.

Keep the Future in Mind

Occasionally I get the opportunity to talk with a young adult about life. They sometimes seek my advice about which college to attend, marriage, finances, or about life in general. I'm not an expert, but they sometimes want an older adult to speak into the decisions they are facing.

I always give them one piece of advice: Whatever you do, keep the future in mind. Don't make hasty decisions based solely on what feels good now. Don't postpone your education. Go to school; learn all you can while you can. Procrastination is your enemy, not your friend. Don't spend all your money; save some for unexpected expenses and for retirement. Don't allow your emotions to cause you to sin. If you do, you will live a life of regrets. Decisions have consequences, and often the ones we make emotionally have the worst effect.

Joy, according to Paul, occurs when you realize God made you for a purpose and is working all the affairs of your life to complete that purpose. No, that doesn't mean God made the bad things happen, prompted people to hurt you, or orchestrated natural disasters to punish you. It does mean that God wants to use all the experiences of your life to make you like Jesus and to help you fulfill His purpose for you.

That is why Paul wrote with confidence that he was sure of one thing: "that he who began a good work in you will bring it to completion at the day of Jesus Christ" (Philippians 1:6).

I have a friend who runs in marathons. Regardless of how much he trains, the race is tiring and painful. Most runners quit before they finish. I asked him what his secret was to completing a race.

He said, "Before the race starts, I visit the finish line and stare at it. And I keep that mental image in my mind constantly as I am running." Then he added, "So, when I think about quitting, I keep remembering that with every step I am one step closer to winning."

That was Paul's secret in life. Keep what is ahead in mind. Keep heaven in your thoughts, and remember that God is working in you and through you until then.

Be What You Are

A few years ago, Debbie and I met a young lady who was an outstanding volleyball player. In fact, she made the all-state team in high school and was planning to play at a major college.

Successful athletes work hard to improve. I'm always interested in what motivates them.

She told us that her greatest motivation was the words of her high school coach. Since her earliest days in middle school, she wanted to be a part of the varsity volleyball team. It was her dream. At her school, the members of the varsity team received a special sweatsuit to wear on game days. Embroidered on it was a tiger, the school's mascot.

When she was a freshman, she made the varsity team. She was excited; she had achieved her lifelong dream. On the day that the coach gave her and her other teammates the sweatsuit and their uniform, he said something that changed her commitment to the game.

After handing out the uniforms, he looked at the new players and pointed to the tiger on the sweatsuit. The coach said, "Today you become a tiger. You are as much a tiger as the best player on the team. But your challenge every day is to be what you are."

Her words ring in my thoughts still. As a believer, you are as much of a saint as Paul was. But the challenge for every Christian—what produces a wellspring of joy—is being what you are created to be.

When Paul wrote his opening remarks to the Philippians, he knew their joy was sure if they continued maturing in their walk with God and fulfilling their purpose.

Love

Nothing demonstrates a believer is growing in their spiritual life like expressions of love. In fact, the apostle John wrote that the absence of love is evidence that one is not a true Christian.

For Paul, the increasing ability to love is a sign of a maturing faith. That is why he expressed in his prayer for the believers in Philippi that their "love may abound more and more" (Philippians 1:9).

Christian love is expressed two ways: toward God and toward others. An easy way to remember these two expressions is to remember the cross—the highest demonstration of love in human history. The cross has a vertical beam and a horizontal beam. The vertical beam reminds us to love God and the horizontal beam reminds us to love others.

People who chase happiness instead of pursuing their purpose think they can love God and despise some people, while others think they can love people and despise God. But the two are inseparable if you want meaning and joy in life. The apostle John, who understood and wrote much about love, connected the two by writing, "If anyone says, 'I love God,' and hates his brother, he is a liar; for he who does not love his brother whom he has seen cannot love God whom he has not seen" (1 John 4:20).

Love isn't an emotion that you force yourself to have. It isn't tolerating everything and everybody. And it is not an excuse for poor decisions or allowing people to misuse you. Love is the result of a life surrendered to God's plan. It is you fulfilling the mission of glorifying God by obeying His commandments and His purpose for you. It is being concerned for the welfare of others—even being willing to sacrifice for them to see their lives improved. It is forgiving others when they offend you, and it is caring enough to desire the best for them. It is acting in their best interest, not yours.

Love in the purest sense isn't natural. It is supernatural. It is the Holy Spirit living through you as you commit your life to Christ. That is why Paul listed love in the fruit of the Spirit in Galatians 5:22. It is interesting to note that Paul listed joy second, because love always precedes joy.

Nothing demonstrates faith like love.

Discernment

Spiritual discernment is the ability to love people in a way that helps them, rather than harming them. It is choosing what is best, rather than what is convenient.

I discovered this truth several years ago when our ministry began working with church planters in New England. Often, a larger church in the South or Midwest wanted to help a new church in the Northeast. With the best of intentions, they did everything for them. They provided the workers for Vacation Bible School. They sent a crew to build their church building. When a financial crisis arose, they sent a check.

However, instead of helping, they were hurting. The members of the new church failed to assume leadership and responsibility. They just relied on someone else to do it for them. And when the sponsoring church ceased to help, the new church closed.

As a believer, giving gives you pleasure. But joy comes from loving and giving with discernment. Paul expressed in his prayer for the love of the Philippians to continue to grow "with knowledge and all discernment, so that you may approve what is excellent" (Philippians 1:9-10).

Like every good parent knows, love isn't giving every person what they want, when they want it, and how they want it. It is using biblical wisdom to make decisions that are best for the person involved. This knowledge comes from studying the Bible. Insight and perception come from applying what you know from Scripture to your life and decisions.

Priorities

When the Holy Spirit inspired the biblical writers to pen words, every word or phrase was carefully selected. Such is the case when Paul added that their love and maturity enabled them to "approve what is excellent" (Philippians 1:10).

Love and discernment allow you to test your actions and your priorities. It should test your actions to help you know what is right or wrong and what you should or should not do. But it also tests your priorities, to show if they are good or the best.

You can live a morally clean life, have wonderful relationships, and be admired, yet lack purpose. These are good things but not the best. The best—or excellent things as Paul described them—are the things you prioritize based on your life's mission statement.

Joy comes from being motivated by your mission and prioritizing the activities that fulfill your purpose. And joy comes from the freedom to say "no" to the good things that keep you from your purpose and the excellent things God desires for you.

Godliness

There is a direct relationship between the joy you feel and the purity in your life. Sin may be fun for a brief time, but the consequences bring lasting pain.

Christians are redeemed from sin because of Christ. When your sin is forgiven, God can't see your sin anymore. But we aren't perfect. Christians struggle with temptation and often violate God's standard of righteousness. Your goal is to be "pure and blameless." In the New Testament, these words describe a godly life. It implies a character that can withstand the scrutiny of bright sunlight.

Several years ago, I spoke in a church in west Alabama. A family in the church invited me, the guest musician, and the pastor to dinner in their home before the service. It was a wonderful meal in a beautiful home.

The guest musician was an elderly gentleman who was extremely talented. And he was known for wearing a white suit, complete with a white shirt and white tie, when he sang. As we were eating, everyone commented on his wardrobe.

Near the end of the meal, I accidentally hit a glass of iced tea, and it emptied into the musician's lap. I immediately grabbed a napkin, and the host got some rags to clean the spill. I was embarrassed. But I was more concerned about the possible stain on his white suit!

Moments later, he assured me that there was no stain. Everyone looked closely, and we agreed.

A brief time later, we left the home and drove to the church. As we walked across the parking lot, I looked at the guest musician. I suddenly stopped. Clearly outlined on his jacket, shirt, tie and pants was one large tea stain! Because it was summer, the sun was brightly shining. We now could see what we could not see in the home where we ate.

Fortunately, he wasn't upset. He laughed about it and even told the congregation what happened. But the experience left an impression on me. What may not be visible to some becomes clear when exposed to direct sunlight. Your Christian life isn't what people see in some places. It is what you are when exposed to the light of God's Word.

When people desire something more than happy, they tend to see joy as a set of actions or attitudes. And joy involves both. But joy must have a foundation of godliness and character to build upon, or all the right actions will never produce it.

Personal Application

You may be asking at this point, why am I listing all the details about remembering and living a godly life? Every builder knows the foundation is the most important part of a house. And godliness is the most important part of a life filled with joy.

Take a moment to reflect on your life. Remember what the Bible says about you as a Christian. Stop trying to be someone else, or what someone else wants you to be. Overcome your insecurity by being who God created you to be.

What changes do you need to make to be more like Jesus? Write the answers as a list, and beside each one, describe how you can incorporate this attribute into your life.

When you do, joy results.

Truth to REMEMBER

Joy starts with who you are,

not with what you do.

CHAPTER 4

Purpose Offers PERSPECTIVE

I want you to know, brothers, that what has happened to me has really served to advance the gospel.

Philippians 1:12

On a cold winter morning, my administrative assistant buzzed my office to tell me I had a phone call. The caller was Keith, a lifelong friend who grew up a short distance from my home. Although he is a few years younger, he and his brothers attended the same school I did. Keith pursued his dream of being a teacher and coach, eventually becoming the principal of the high school we attended.

As I answered the phone, we took a few minutes to catch up with the news about our families, and then he asked me, "Phil, would you be willing to be the speaker for our graduation in May?"

"Well, of course, I will," I replied without hesitation. Then I added, "I will if I only have to speak between five and seven minutes." I knew from experience that no one attends a graduation to hear the speaker. They all sit politely, wondering when the speaker will end so they can watch their child or grandchild receive their diploma.

"That will be fine," Keith said with a chuckle. "You know time is important at these events."

After I hung up the phone, I thought how honored I felt. Then I started thinking about what I would say. I called Keith a few days later and asked if I could stop by the school. I didn't have an agenda. I wanted to give him my thoughts and see if they met his expectations.

I arrived on campus, checked into the office, and was told Keith was in a meeting that was running late. I asked permission to wander the hallways and was given a guest pass. Keith, I was told, would text me when he ended the meeting.

West Morgan School consisted of all grades, first through twelfth. I went to the same building from the day I entered until I graduated. One long hallway held the rooms for elementary students and another for middle and high school.

Memories flooded my mind as I walked the hallways. I thought of childhood friends who moved away and wondered how life was for them. And I remembered the teachers that molded my life into the person I am today.

But something was different. The gym I thought seated thousands really seated hundreds. The cafeteria I thought could feed the whole student body contained only a fraction of the chairs as it had when I was there. And the hallway that appeared to be a mile long when I was in the first grade was now an easy walk.

I remember thinking, "This place has changed!"

The bell rang, and students hurried from one classroom to the next. A few minutes later, it was quiet in the hallways again. And then I realized where the change occurred.

The gym seated the same number of people as it did when I was there. The cafeteria did too. And the hallways were the same length. The only change from my days in this building was me.

When I was in school, this was my world. Sure, I had a wonderful family, and we were a part of a church, but school was the place where I faced the big challenges in my life. Challenges like forgetting my lunch money in the first grade and wondering what I should do. Or a girl I liked in middle school pointing out that my clothes didn't match. Or feeling that life was over when our basketball team lost the championship game.

When I think about those things, they make me smile. None of them mattered in the big picture of my life. Looking back, they weren't as life altering as I thought. You see, I have a new perspective about life and problems. I now view my negative school experiences from a broader perspective. I put them in the bigger context of what is happening in my life and the world around me.

The Bigger Context

When you see your mission in life is to glorify God, and you start fulfilling the purpose God has for you, you start to view everything that happens around you and to you differently. You start seeing life from an eternal perspective.

Nothing affects our lives and our emotions like our perspective. When I was in the first grade, lacking lunch money rocked my world. I cried. When a girl mentioned how bad my clothes were, I didn't want to go to school and certainly didn't want to see her or her friends. And when the basketball team lost, I never wanted to see a basketball again. I remember thinking, "Who wants a stupid trophy anyway?"

But what if I had the perspective then that I have now as an adult? I would be able to see that all those experiences were preparing me for life. Maybe I needed to learn the importance of preparation by making sure I had my lunch money before I left for school. Or that some people will criticize or bully us because they are dealing with their own personal struggles. And learning how to lose is as important as learning how to win.

I realized early in my ministry that the wrong perspective naturally leads to a bad attitude. When a man gripes about his wife not meeting his needs, I know that he fails to understand marriage isn't about getting your needs met. It is about meeting the needs of your spouse, even if they don't reciprocate. When a person is complaining about their church singing the wrong music or not spending money as they desire, I know they have a self-focused perspective.

And when you have a wrong perspective about life—that is, a view of life that is not based on a biblical mission statement—you will fall victim to the greatest joy-killers of all.

Satan's plan is to distract you from your purpose by changing how you look at life. He wants you to believe that there is something better, and that God's plan for you isn't the best.

Remember what Satan told Eve in the Garden of Eden? God's desire for them was to live in a perfect environment. Their only responsibility was to care for the garden and to obey Him by avoiding fruit from the tree of the knowledge of good and evil. That was their mission and purpose. But Satan diverted their attention. He changed their perspective. He convinced them that there was something better than God's plan for their life. And they listened. As a result, they brought sin into the world and had to leave the Garden of Eden forever.

Satan continually tries to refocus your attention. He points out what others are or what they have, trying to get you to abandon your mission to glorify God.

Through my years of ministry, I've met many people who experienced similar experiences in life—often bad experiences that affected everything from relationships to their financial stability. The places or people may change, but the core experiences are the same.

The experiences left some filled with joy and others filled with bitterness. But why? What was the difference between two people experiencing similar situations and responding in two different ways?

The difference was perspective.

The Victim

Many people see themselves as a victim. Their problems are the result of circumstances beyond their control, or perhaps they feel that people took advantage of them. And they use these situations or people as an excuse for their bitterness. Before long, a victim mentality allows anyone to justify every negative choice in his or her life—everything from laziness and irresponsibility to revenge and crime.

It is true some people are harmed by the actions of others. And some people are given a favored starting point because of their family, race, or gender. Still others are preferred because they have natural good looks or athletic abilities. It happens.

I confess that I have found myself feeling or thinking like a victim when something doesn't go my way. It is easy to say, "That's not fair!"

And I've also discovered that the devil is more than ready to supply an excuse if it keeps me from glorifying God! The excuse Satan provides can consume your thoughts, destroying your joy in the process, and keeping you from fulfilling what God put you on earth to do.

The Survivor

Survivors, too, may face pain that they didn't deserve. Someone didn't treat them fairly. Maybe they, too, were overlooked for a promotion at work because they weren't as attractive, or they didn't have the right skin color.

Survivors, however, are different from victims. Victims feel they deserve better. They are quick to blame others. They feel entitled to something more. But survivors react differently. Instead of blaming others or circumstances, they accept what comes their way, hoping they can get through life without more hurt and pain. Survivors lack self-worth because they can't see themselves as God does—as a forgiven, redeemed child of His.

Survivors don't lash out or express anger. They exist. They go through daily activities, doing the least that life requires. Survivors lack purpose, and they certainly lack joy.

The Conqueror

Both victims and survivors chase happiness, but when they can't find it in people or things, they assume life is a matter of luck or privilege. They assume success only comes when people are in the right place at the right time. Or they assume their success comes from being born into a wealthy family. And, of course, they think success will bring the happiness they want.

People who know their God-given purpose understand that isn't true. They know a meaningful life comes from having a personal relationship with Jesus Christ, finding the assignments He has, and trusting Him as they do them.

People die. Circumstances can change in a few seconds. But a relationship with Christ is sure, and nothing can take it away. As a result, people with a purpose can overcome anything that has happened.

People with a purpose can overcome anything that has happened.

From Victim to Conqueror

One of my heroes is George Washington Carver. If anyone was a victim, it was him. Carver was born to two slaves in Missouri during the Civil War. When he was an infant, some evil men kidnapped him, along with his mother and his sister. The men took them to Kentucky and sold them to other slave owners. Carver never saw his mother and sister again.

His original owner hired a man to find the family and bring them home. He found only George, and he brought him back to Missouri.

As a child, Carver was sick often. When he was 13, he watched a group of white men in Fort Scott, Kansas, kill a black man. But he refused to let this destroy him. He found a way to go to school—several schools, in fact—until he graduated from high school. This was an almost impossible task for an African-American at that time in American history.

After being accepted into college because of his grades, Carver was refused entry the day he arrived because the school hadn't known that he was black when he registered.

By now, Carver had every reason to become bitter, but he didn't. Instead, he bought 17 acres and raised garden produce to save money for more education.

In 1891, he was the first black student at Iowa State University. Carver excelled in botany and obtained his master's degree in 1896. Later, he became the first black faculty member at Iowa State. When Booker T. Washington started Tuskegee Institute, which later became Tuskegee University, he asked Carver to head the agricultural division.

For the next 47 years, Carver devoted his life to researching and teaching students about plants. His research into crops such as peanuts, soybeans, and sweet potatoes continues to be used today. Some historians believe that his research into the importance of crop rotation improved the agricultural output of Southern farmers in the early 1900s.

George Washington Carver never saw himself as a victim or a survivor. He was a conqueror. But do you know why? When Carver was ten years old, he gave his life to Jesus Christ. Carver accepted who and what God said he was, not what a bigoted society was telling him.

From his childhood, George Washington Carver lived to glorify God in his life. Scientific research was his "what," his divine purpose, but glorifying God was his "why."

God's Perspective

When Paul wrote to the Christians in Philippi, his desire was for them to fulfill their purpose and know real joy in the process. He knew they would seek happiness, but it would never satisfy the deepest longings of their hearts. For Paul, the basis of a fulfilling life was knowing how God views you—as a forgiven child of His creation, made to glorify Him by fulfilling His purpose for you.

Paul challenged the church to approach problems, challenges, and struggles from God's viewpoint. Instead of seeing things you can't control from your limited perspective, Paul said to look at them from God's perspective. After all, God sees current issues and your role in them on an eternal time line.

When I was an elementary student, I would tell my mother about my struggles. She would tell me to trust her that someone making a rude comment wasn't the end of my life. She countered my immature perspective with a mature one. I trusted her. Time proved my mother was right, and in the same way, our Heavenly Father wants us to trust His eternal perspective.

The Philippians, meanwhile, had one big question for Paul: Why was he in prison? Wasn't God powerful enough to set him free? Wouldn't Paul be able to do more for Christ if he was out of jail rather than in it?

The believers in Philippi could legitimately ask those questions because they knew God had freed him once before. And great good had come from it.

As a missionary, Paul focused his attention on areas where Jews were open to the idea of Jesus being the Messiah. His preaching angered traditionalists, but many people accepted the gospel message. During his second missionary journey, Paul and those with him stopped in Troas. One night, Paul saw a vision from God telling him to go to Macedonia, a province of the Roman Empire in Greece.

Paul obeyed. It was the first time anyone came to Europe to share the good news of salvation.

After arriving in the seaport town of Neapolis, Paul and Silas traveled inland about ten miles to Philippi. Before these trips, Paul normally went to the Jewish synagogue and spoke. But in Philippi there wasn't a synagogue. Instead, they found a group of women praying by the river.

Paul and Silas joined the group and shared the gospel. As a result, a local merchant named Lydia became a follower of Christ. Her family followed. And a female slave whose owner made her practice fortune-telling also did. This young girl was possessed by a demon, but Paul commanded the demon to leave. Her owners, seeing the financial loss, demanded that Paul and Silas be beaten and put in jail.

But Paul and Silas weren't victims or survivors. They knew that they were doing what God told them to do and, by doing it, they were fulfilling their life's mission of glorifying God. So, amid their pain, they started singing.

Even in the worst circumstances, joy will find a way to express itself if people are doing what God calls them to do. And while they were singing, a major earthquake shook the ground. The force broke down the walls of the jail, and all the prisoners were able to escape. The jailer, assuming the prisoners were gone and knowing he would be blamed, decided to commit suicide.

Paul stopped him.

At that moment, the jailer realized that Paul and Silas possessed something he did not. And he knew that he wanted it. After Paul shared the gospel with him, the jailer and his family became Christians. Many historians believe that the jailer's family and Lydia's family were among the founding members of the church in Philippi. In addition, others came to Christ, probably having heard of how God miraculously freed Paul and Silas.

Years later, Paul arrived in Rome. The uproar from his words resulted in his arrest. While sitting in a prison cell, he wrote to his friends in Philippi. He knew what they were wondering: *Why was Paul in jail? And why didn't God send another earthquake to set him free?*

Sincere questions deserve honest answers. And Paul's answer? They needed a new perspective on the problem. They needed God's perspective. Paul reminded the Philippians of his mission and purpose in life. He glorified God by sharing the gospel and establishing churches. Sometimes God used miraculous acts to accomplish His plan. But miracles weren't the mission. Paul's purpose was to share the gospel.

> *Miracles weren't the mission. Paul's purpose was to share the gospel.*

With that perspective in mind, Paul believed that his imprisonment was accomplishing that purpose. It "really served to advance the gospel" (Philippians 1:12). In writing this, Paul used a Greek military term that referred to an advance team, like modern engineers, who prepared a way for the soldiers to enter a new territory. For Paul, preaching in a Roman prison opened a new area for the gospel to be shared. It was a different kind of victory.

His purpose was to share the gospel and establish churches. Sometimes, God used miracles to do it. Other times, God used suffering to open hearts to hear. Either way, God acted in the best interest of the mission.

The Way to Purpose May Be Through Suffering

Shortly after Debbie and I married, my father had a heart attack. Tests revealed that three major arteries around his heart were blocked. The only way to prolong his life was bypass surgery. The doctors sawed his sternum, pulled his ribs back, stopped his heart, harvested arteries from his leg, performed the triple bypass, wired his sternum together, and closed the incision.

It hurt. For nearly six weeks my father couldn't move or breathe without discomfort. But suffering was necessary to heal his body.

Many times, for you to glorify God and fulfill your purpose, you will suffer. It won't always be comfortable. Paul certainly wasn't comfortable in prison as he awaited trial. Important prisoners awaiting trial before Caesar had a guard chained to them 24 hours a day. Each guard had a six-hour shift. That meant every day Paul had the chance to share Jesus with four different soldiers! Men, I might add, who couldn't go anywhere.

Some soldiers became believers. But it didn't stop there. The legal authorities would hear the gospel, too, when they heard and reviewed Paul's appeal.

Confidence in God Encourages Others

Have you noticed a discouraged person easily discourages people around them? But the opposite is also true. Encouragement encourages encouragement.

Now, Paul wasn't the only Christian in Rome. Some were discouraged because of persecution. They probably fell for the temptation to see what God wasn't doing rather than what He was doing. But Paul's boldness and his willingness to stay true to his life's mission encouraged them. Paul said, because of his imprisonment, these discouraged believers were "much more bold to speak the word without fear" (Philippians 1:14).

Paul had a choice. He could see his chains, or he could see an opportunity to fulfill his purpose. He could think that God owed him a miracle because of his sacrifice, or he could be grateful for the salvation he had through Christ.

Paul could have pouted, complained, and become bitter. But he didn't. Paul had an eternal perspective. He saw things from God's viewpoint. And, as a result, he never lost his joy.

Personal Application

How you view life and how you view what happens in life is your perspective. You choose to see life from God's viewpoint or yours.

You can rejoice in what God is doing and have joy. Or you can be upset about what He is not doing and be unhappy. You can focus on your purpose, or you can be upset with everyone around you. It is your choice.

Paul had the same choice. He chose to fulfill what God called him to do and let God handle everything else. It resulted in him having joy.

Take a few moments to read the first chapter of Philippians in the Bible. Notice how Paul stayed on mission, not allowing bad things or bad people to control him.

Truth to REMEMBER

When you are living with purpose, you are excited about what God is doing. You refuse to allow circumstances or people to destroy your purpose.

CHAPTER 5

Purpose Overcomes
PAIN

*It is my eager expectation and hope that I
will not be at all ashamed, but that with full
courage now as always Christ will be honored
in my body, whether by life or by death. For
to me to live is Christ, and to die is gain.*

Philippians 1:20-21

September 12, 2020, was coming up. I was dreading its arrival. There wasn't anything unusual on my calendar. No doctor's appointment. No difficult meetings. Even close friends didn't realize that there was anything different about that day.

But I knew.

On that day, I turned 60 years old.

For some people, that might not be a crisis, but for me it was. When I turned 40, I was teased about it. I got the party where people grieved the death of my youth. Turning 50 came and went without much thought given to aging.

But turning 60 was emotionally challenging. I realized that I was making the turn to start the final lap in life. Sure, I expect to live many more years, but I was keenly aware that the next few years would probably be filled with more pain than pleasure. It is part of getting old.

When Debbie and I were in our twenties, we went to the hospital often to celebrate the birth of a child. We rarely went to the funeral home to grieve the death of a friend.

In our forties, we began to experience suffering in a new way. Doctors diagnosed Debbie's father with inoperable cancer. He died three months later. Her mother later died of a blood disease. A short time after, my father died instantly of a heart attack.

By our late fifties, all our parents were gone. Two died in their sixties and one in their early seventies. Only my mother lived into her eighties.

To remind us of our aging, we, too, began to have health issues. Fortunately, none of them are life threatening, but we know that the older we get, the more quickly that can change.

Time makes you aware of suffering. Pain no longer comes as a surprise or a stranger. And suffering can occur at any age and without any warning. Maybe it is a visit to a doctor's office that changes your world forever. Or maybe it is a notice from your employer, a call from your investment adviser, or your spouse telling you he or she is leaving.

When pain comes into your life, if your mission isn't clear and you aren't committed to God's purpose and plan for your life, it will destroy you emotionally, spiritually, and sometimes physically. Pain will expose whether you are chasing happiness or pursuing your purpose. Suffering removes all the insincere smiles to show the tears in your heart. And it reveals the difference between happiness and the joy that comes from living with purpose.

- Happiness depends on a sunny day. Joy sees a rainy day as a chance to see a rainbow or to watch the flowers grow.

- Happiness depends upon a perfect body that is in perfect health. Joy allows you to accept imperfections as gifts from God to glorify Him in an imperfect world.

- Happiness depends upon never losing anyone you love. Joy rejoices in the time you had together and looks forward to a home in heaven.

- Happiness depends upon winning. Joy sees losing as an opportunity to be stronger and better.

- Happiness says, "I like life if people like me." Joy says, "Life is good because God loves me."

- Happiness is temporary. Joy is eternal.

- Happiness sees death as the end, but joy sees it as the beginning.

People often want to be told what they want to hear. But a doctor isn't your friend if she says you're fine when the cancer is growing inside you. Or a banker tells you that your credit is good when he knows you'll be turned down for every loan. Or a boss tells you your job is secure...only to inform you the next day that your position is being terminated.

And a minister who refuses to tell you the truth about life isn't your friend either. So here is the truth I've learned in 60 years of living: You will have disappointments. Life will throw you for a loop. People will hurt you. And if Jesus doesn't return soon, you and everyone you love will die.

But before you let that thought depress you, be encouraged. In the middle of every situation or hurt, you can have joy. Not a superficial, fake happiness, but real joy—a joy that comes from knowing that God has it all under control and knew what would happen when He created and designed you for a purpose.

> *Pain will expose whether you are chasing happiness or pursuing your purpose.*

Win-Win

As we discussed in the previous chapter, when Paul wrote to the Philippians, he emphasized commitment to God's purpose, viewing everything from His perspective. That's easy to do when life is good, but when pain becomes personal, it is up to you to choose between your worldly happiness and your eternal purpose.

For Paul, the pain of being in prison was personal. Modern prisons are not nice places, but a Roman prison nearly 2,000 years ago was almost unbearable. Prisoners were tied up, making movement almost impossible. Often their arms and legs were chained to a wall or a permanent structure. Can you imagine sitting or lying 24 hours a day with limited sunshine, horrible food to eat, and no way to practice personal hygiene?

To make matters worse, what if you knew it was only a few days until your head would be severed from your body in one of the cruelest forms of execution?

Yet, in this Roman cell, Paul wrote, "I will rejoice" (Philippians 1:18).

In business negotiations, the best deals occur when each side can determine what the other side wants and present a plan to help them achieve it, while also getting what they want. It is called a win-win because no one loses.

Paul knew his situation was serious. Death was a real possibility any day. He wasn't happy about it, but he had joy. For Paul, living or dying was a win-win situation. His purpose was for Christ to be honored, or magnified, in his body—"whether by life or by death" (Philippians 1:20). Out of that commitment, Paul gave us one of the most powerful verses in the Bible, Philippians 1:21: "For to me to live is Christ, and to die is gain." In his sincere encouragement for the church to remain faithful, Paul spoke from his heart.

Keep Heaven in Mind

Paul had a unique perspective on dying for the cause of Christ. When he was opposed to Christianity in his early adult life, he witnessed the execution of Stephen. Paul may have helped with the stoning. While Stephen was dying, he looked toward the sky and saw Jesus standing at the right hand of God.

We don't know if Paul saw it, but he knew Stephen saw something. The vision allowed Stephen to endure the pain to gain something better. Stephen couldn't have realized how his commitment to God would affect Paul...and how the life and death of Paul, in turn, would affect the early church.

When something bad happens, your response will reveal your commitment to magnifying God, and it will determine how much joy you experience, both now and in the future. Pain will affect you in one of three ways: You can let it destroy your joy, you can allow it to control you emotionally, or you can grow from it.

> *You can let pain destroy you,*
> *control you, or grow you.*

Destroy You

People who are chasing happiness will be emotionally destroyed when suffering comes, especially if the pain alters their lifestyle.

Several years ago, I met a young, successful businessman when I was speaking in his city. From the day he graduated from college, everything he touched, it seemed, turned to gold. He was smart, articulate, and had a winsome personality to boot. People were drawn to him.

Shortly after I connected with him, a business acquaintance told him about a new investment opportunity. The acquaintance was making more money in a month than the young man's investments were returning in a year. He knew this was the chance to become wealthy, have everything he wanted, and retire early. Against the counsel of his accountant, he invested most of his financial assets in the new venture. Six months later, the founder was indicted for running a Ponzi scheme. He lost it all.

Depression consumed him. Feeling hopeless, he took his life.

Most people who experience a setback won't take their own lives. But something about them dies—their dreams, their plans, their joy. That is, they cease to live life to the fullest. These people were chasing happiness, and when pain came, there was no reason to live.

Control You

Debbie and I recall a lady we met one night after I spoke in her church. She probably was in her midseventies. From the moment we met her, she never smiled.

After talking with her, we learned that her husband left her a few years earlier. She discovered a love note from his secretary. When she confronted him about the affair, he chose to live with the other woman. Divorce followed, along with the loss of the lifestyle afforded by her husband's high-income job.

Regardless of what we said, she felt hopeless. Her pain made her look and act like a corpse. She relived the affair and the emotions she felt every day. It was like a movie that would begin every morning and play until she went to sleep.

Every conversation made its way to her sharing her pain. Friends started avoiding the woman because her pain controlled her. So, in a way, her husband's sin destroyed her too. Instead of seeing hope, she chose to let her painful experience control her thoughts, her conversations, and her life.

Grow You

The difference between a person chasing happiness and someone pursuing their purpose is how they process pain. People fulfilling their God-given assignments see pain as another way to magnify the Lord in their lives.

One of the most remarkable women I've ever met is Joni Eareckson Tada. When Joni was 17 years old, she went swimming in Chesapeake Bay. When she dove into the water, she misjudged the depth. Instead of being deep, the water was shallow. She fractured her back between the fourth and fifth cervical levels. Although she lived, she became a quadriplegic, paralyzed from her shoulders down.

At first, the injury almost destroyed her emotionally. She admitted in her autobiography that she was angry and depressed. But she came to realize that she was created for a purpose: to glorify God through a ministry that encouraged people, especially people with a disability.

Joni certainly didn't choose disability. She didn't wish for the divine assignment. But she embraced the change that suffering brought into her life. Since her injury, Joni has become an artist. She learned to paint by holding a brush between her teeth. She has written over 40 books, recorded musical albums, starred in a movie about her life, and became a vocal advocate for people with disabilities.

Did Joni wish for the pain? No.

Was God punishing her? No.

Several years ago, I heard Joni speak. She addressed the suffering she experienced. And she answered the two questions everyone in the audience was wondering: *Why doesn't God remove suffering from the world? And why wasn't she upset that God didn't heal her?*

I remember her answers. "If God removed suffering, He would have to remove sin," Joni said. "If He removed sin, He would have to return. And if He returned, others could not be saved."

Then she added, "I am willing to postpone my healing to see others come to Christ."

Today, Joni has joy because she found her purpose in her pain, and that purpose magnifies God in her life.

Evidence of Trust

After Paul told the Philippians that he was in a win-win situation with his suffering, he reminded them how a person committed to glorifying God wins, regardless of the suffering they experience. If Paul died, he would be with Jesus. But if he lived, he could continue his ministry. Either way, Paul wins. The present pain is only a door to something deeper, richer, and more fulfilling.

Athletes know it. They often remind themselves, "No pain, no gain."

Surgeons know it. No pain, no healing.

And believers should know it. There are some things you only learn through suffering, and we can see through the pain to something better:

- Pain tests your sincerity. That is why Paul challenged the Christians in Philippi to "let your manner of life be worthy of the gospel of Christ" (Philippians 1:27).

- Pain can cause you to be disagreeable. You become inwardly angry because you are hurting, and you take that anger out on others. It's often been said that hurting people hurt people. And if you are only seeking happiness, your pain will cause you to hurt others. Maybe that is why Paul urged the Philippians to be on their guard, so they would be "standing firm in one spirit, with one mind striving side by side for the faith of the gospel" (Philippians 1:27).

- Pain can cause you to live in fear, uncertain of the future, if you aren't living by your mission statement to glorify God. That is why Paul said the Philippians should not be afraid of anything the world, their enemies, or the devil throws at them. Because their lack of fear was evidence of their trust in God.

- Pain is a powerful force to people chasing happiness because it can destroy everything in a second. Happiness always walks out when pain enters a room. Joy, when it comes from your purpose, doesn't leave unless we ask it to.

Personal Application

Nothing worthwhile comes without difficulty and pain. And your spiritual life is no different.

Take a piece of paper and write about the most painful experience in your life or the most painful struggle you presently have. Write about the ways it makes you feel.

Now read it.

Are you angry because the pain destroyed your happiness or your concept of happiness? Are you allowing your pain to destroy you or control you emotionally? Is there anything this struggle taught you?

Read what you wrote one more time, but this time, ask your Heavenly Father how your pain can fulfill His purpose. How can God be glorified through it?

Truth to REMEMBER

Painful experiences destroy people chasing happiness. People living with a purpose keep pain in check, refusing to allow it to control them, and use it as a launching pad for something better.

CHAPTER 6

Purpose Produces SECURITY

Being found in human form, he humbled himself by becoming obedient to the point of death, even death on a cross.

Philippians 2:8

I n my travels, I've met thousands of people. Occasionally a person stands above the rest—not because of their size, personality, or achievements, but because they possess a quiet strength that is not offensive or repulsive. Their life isn't filled with drama. They have an inner peace—an assurance of their purpose and a dedication to it. Gossip doesn't torment them. Braggers don't intimidate them. And insecure people long to be like them.

Sitting in a restaurant in Missouri several years ago, I met a man who exemplified this trait. I spoke in his church on a Sunday morning, and some mutual friends invited several couples to join us for lunch.

One gentleman seated near me took a keen interest in our ministry. His questions about our work had a way of affirming what we do. Later, I turned the conversation to his line of work.

"Tell me, what do you do?"

"Oh, I'm just a schoolteacher," he responded.

"Just a schoolteacher?" I replied. "I think schoolteachers are the most important people in the world!" I wanted to validate his work and let him know that I appreciated his impact on young lives.

He smiled and said, "Oh, I totally agree with you. Teaching and molding lives is so important." Before I could ask what subject he taught, our food arrived, and soon everyone was eating a delicious meal.

Later that afternoon, I wanted to write him and his wife a personal note to express how much I enjoyed our time. I did a quick Internet search to find his address. The results startled me. My jaw literally dropped, and my eyes widened. I could not believe what I was seeing. The man who was "just a schoolteacher" was the president of a major university. And he was being considered for the position of Secretary of Education in the cabinet of the president of the United States!

That evening I saw him again, and I had to ask. "Why didn't you tell me who you were?"

His reply is one that I will always remember: "It wasn't important. What was important was hearing about you and your ministry."

The character trait was in plain sight: humility. Having a purpose gives you emotional security, and that sense of security causes you to be humble. Because you are secure in who and whose you are, you don't need to set yourself above any other person. And humility is attractive.

> *Your purpose brings emotional security, and that sense of security causes you to be humble.*

Diagnosing Insecurity

At first, you may be drawn to an individual who seems confident. But the more time you spend with them, the more you realize that the confidence is a front. The real person underneath is deeply insecure about who or what he or she is.

Insecure people tend to display four characteristics:

Self-Made Heroes

Insecure people fear rejection. They are uncomfortable with who they are, so they try to elevate themselves before others. And the best way to do it is to tell stories where they are always the hero. If you pause for a moment, you may realize that you've heard one today.

"The place was a mess before I got here."

"They had problems that they couldn't handle, so they brought me in."

"The kids told me they would've lost the game if it hadn't been for me."

Always the hero.

Quick to Gossip

Insecure people fear not being in the know, and they get a thrill from knowing something others don't. And the thrill comes from being the first to tell. For that reason, gossiping is one of their favorite pastimes. Knowledge is power to them.

They live to talk on the phone because it prompts others to tell them inside information in exchange for what they know. And, if necessary, they can use their knowledge to privately control situations. But gossip is...

- a form of judging. It causes you to give an opinion of another person's choices or actions.

- a form of blackmail. You feel empowered by revealing what you know, thereby lowering someone's esteem in the eyes of your listener.

- a way to keep from revealing your heart. By talking about another person, you hope no one sees you for what you are.

Easily Offended

Insecure people get their feelings hurt...a lot!

They are wounded because they weren't asked to participate, or they were asked not to participate. A younger, more inexperienced person got the promotion instead of them, or someone criticized them and their work.

The offense comes from being rejected, being known for who they really are rather than who they pretend to be. Another person rained on their imaginary parade and exposed them as fake.

Always a Critic

If their stories don't convince you how wonderful they are, maybe their insights will. For an insecure person, nothing is perfect—except, in some cases, themselves. They cannot compliment another person without a word of "constructive" criticism. Deep inside, they think they are helping, but they are seeking approval. If only you could see how wise they are!

It is one thing to be bold when the enemy you are facing clearly is defined as someone who opposes you. But what about someone who claims to be your friend, your partner in ministry, or your teammate? Nothing challenges your perspective like another Christian criticizing you. It causes you to lose focus and to start doubting your purpose.

Some teachers in Rome and elsewhere were jealous of Paul. They envied his influence among Christians. They viewed him as a rival. But Paul didn't allow his Christian critics to change his perspective.

Instead, he acknowledged the obvious: They "preach Christ from envy and rivalry" (Philippians 1:15).

Perhaps Satan has tried to rob your joy by trying to make you act as the Holy Spirit for other people. You feel it is your mission to correct everyone in the church and set the record straight about everything. There is a place and a biblical process for dealing with Christians living with open sin. But it rarely is the sin of other Christians that defeats our joy. It is personality conflicts, jealousy, or envy that does it. In other words, we lose our joy when we are doing the right thing for the wrong reason. We get too focused on how God is handling these people and what He is going to do with them.

After the resurrection, Jesus had a conversation with Peter. He asked Peter three times if he loved Him, and three times Peter responded that he did. Then Jesus told Peter how he would be persecuted and martyred for his faith.

A few minutes later, John walked up behind them. Peter asked Jesus, "What about him?" Jesus said for Peter not to worry about John. If God wanted John to live until Christ returned, Peter shouldn't allow it to affect him (John 21:15-22).

Jealousy will destroy your joy and keep you from your purpose. Fortunately, Paul offered a remedy: Keep looking at the good people. Instead of thinking about those preaching for the wrong reasons, think about those who are doing it for the right reasons. "Some indeed preach Christ from envy and rivalry, but others from good will. The latter do it out of love, knowing that I am put here for the defense of the gospel" (Philippians 1:15-16). Paul chose to see the good people, not the bad ones.

Paul took biblical truth seriously. But he never took his critics seriously. He certainly never permitted them to distract his focus or destroy his joy. In fact, Paul knew the power was in the message, not the messenger. He could say, "Whether in pretense or in truth, Christ is proclaimed, and in that I rejoice" (Philippians 1:18). Never allow your circumstances or your critics to keep you from what God designed you for and called you to do.

A Person with a Purpose

The characteristics and personalities of an insecure person are easily diagnosed. Everyone knows one, or two, or more. The cure is harder to find.

An insecure person is a person without a mission or a purpose. Imagine for a moment that the local fire department receives an emergency call. A house is on fire, and two children are trapped inside.

The firefighters grab their equipment, jump into the fire engine, and race to the scene, lights flashing and sirens blaring. When they arrive, they leap from the truck. Each firefighter does what he is trained to do. One connects the hose to a hydrant while another adjusts the water pressure. Two put on oxygen tanks and quickly make their way into the burning structure while other firefighters shoot water onto the fire.

Moments later, the two firefighters emerge from the house, each with a child in their arms. Medical personnel check the children and determine that they will be fine. Soon the blaze is extinguished. The firefighters accomplished their mission.

But what about the man who called the fire chief's office because the sirens were too loud? Or the lady who wrote the mayor complaining about the fire truck passing her at a high rate of speed? Or the neighbor who didn't like the fire truck blocking his driveway? The firefighters ignored the complaints because they had a mission and a purpose.

Every good fire department wants to improve their skills. They listen to any suggestion, but they will not let criticism deter them from their reason for existing.

Knowing why you are here and having a commitment to your purpose gives you a sense of security that you will never find chasing happiness or pleasing others.

Humility Starts in the Mind

Paul wanted the Christians in Philippi to know joy—a joy that flows from inside. One that, unlike happiness, is not dependent on internal factors. It is a joy that comes from understanding that our mission is to magnify God, and God has given every one of us an assignment to fulfill that mission. And that assignment is our purpose for living.

But pursuing that purpose isn't easy. There is a daily battle between our selfish ego that wants to chase happy, and the surrendering of our will that allows the Holy Spirit to work through us. The first produces pride; the latter, humility.

- Pride likes to win arguments, but humility listens and learns.

- Pride only runs with people who can advance its cause, but humility likes people that pride avoids.

- Pride craves attention. Humility deflects attention.

- Pride feeds on greed. Humility feeds on love.

- Pride says, "I can do anything." Humility says, "Help me."

- Pride is never satisfied, but humility produces contentment.

- The middle letter of pride is *I*. But *U* comes before *I* in humility.

That is why Paul's challenge is a check on our motives. "Do nothing from selfish ambition or conceit, but in humility count others more significant than yourselves. Let each of you look not only to his own interests, but also to the interests of others" (Philippians 2:3-4). Paul understood the battle. He knew what believers needed was a model—a demonstration of someone who knew his purpose, was committed totally to glorifying God, and who fulfilled his mission.

For Paul, there was no greater example than Jesus. Jesus often dealt with an insecure group of people called the Pharisees. They were an arrogant, selfish, racist group of religious people. And they despised Jesus. On one occasion, the disciples told Jesus that the Pharisees were offended by His words. Their offense exposed their insecurity. Jesus, who was secure in who He was and with His purpose, wasn't rattled. He told the disciples to leave them alone. Pandering to insecure people only makes matters worse.

Humility starts in the mind. That is why Paul wrote, "Have this mind among yourselves, which is yours in Christ Jesus" (Philippians 2:5). And that mindset was evident before Jesus came to earth, while He was on earth, and after He returned to heaven.

Before Coming to Earth

The Bible speaks of God the Father, God the Son (Jesus), and God the Holy Spirit. One God expressed in three persons. We call this the Trinity.

That is hard to grasp. Before Jesus came to earth, He was fully God. He didn't start to exist at His birth. He existed for all eternity past. When Jesus was born in Bethlehem, He assumed the limitations of a human body. Jesus didn't feel entitled. He didn't come kicking and screaming. Jesus came willingly and selflessly.

Jesus came humbly.

While on Earth

For 33 years, Jesus lived on earth among people, caring for them and loving them. When He started His earthly ministry, Jesus revealed God through His teaching and His actions. And Jesus modeled humility.

Jesus demonstrated that humility was not being timid. When He saw the abuse of the moneychangers in the temple, He drove them from the area. And Jesus demonstrated that humility wasn't letting people control you. He knew His mission, and His humility kept Him on track. The life of Jesus illustrated how humility was strength under control.

The humility of Jesus came through in His relationships. Humility attracts people because it puts others first. The hurting came because Jesus cared. The children came because He gave them time. The people that society rejected came because He was forgiving.

The primary purpose of Jesus wasn't to teach, although He was a great teacher. His mission wasn't to perform miracles, though He performed many. Jesus came to die for the sins of people everywhere. The cross was the final test of His humility. "Being found in human form, he humbled himself by becoming obedient to the point of death, even death on a cross" (Philippians 2:8).

During His lifetime, people accused Jesus of many things. He was called a drunkard, a glutton, and a blasphemer. But no one, not even His worst critic, ever accused Him of pride.

Return to Heaven

Humility leads to honor, although it doesn't seek it. Without ceasing to be God, Jesus fulfilled His purpose on earth.

Paul, writing about the faithfulness of Christ, said that "God has highly exalted him and bestowed on him the name that is above every name, so that at the name of Jesus every knee should bow, in heaven and on earth and under the earth, and every tongue confess that Jesus Christ is Lord, to the glory of God the Father" (Philippians 2:9-11).

The contrast to Jesus is Satan. Isaiah, the Old Testament prophet, wrote of the time when Satan was thrown from heaven because of his rebellion. And Satan's rebellion was rooted in pride. Numerous times, Isaiah noted that the proud Lucifer said in his heart, "I will" (14:12-14).

But Jesus, in His humility, said, "Not as I will, but as you will" (Matthew 26:39).

Acts of Service

Dr. James Nolan was a longtime friend of our family. I first met him when he treated players from our high school football team. After high school, he and I developed a deep, personal friendship. Dr. Nolan was a man I aspired to be. He was kind, gracious, and humble. He rarely spoke of himself or his dreams. It was always about you when you were in his presence.

When he died unexpectedly, his family asked me to speak at his memorial service. I was honored.

That day, the chapel was filled to overflowing. One by one, people privately shared their stories about his impact on their lives. But all their stories had a unique characteristic. No one, that I recall, spoke of his medical skills. They all related a story about him helping them in another way. He brought food when someone was ill. He mowed an elderly man's lawn. He gave one man a pair of shoes. Oddly enough, his family often didn't know about it.

And Dr. Nolan gave something else too. He gave people time. Time to listen. Time to pray. And when needed, time to help. The lesson from his life was clear: The quickest way to spot a humble person is by their acts of service.

Days before His crucifixion, Jesus gathered His disciples in a room. Normally at gatherings like this, a servant would remove the guests' sandals and wash the dust and dirt from their feet. This time, Jesus took a towel and washed the feet of every disciple, no exceptions. He washed the feet of Judas, who was in the middle of planning his betrayal of Jesus. He washed Peter's feet, knowing that Peter would deny Him in a few hours. And Jesus washed the feet of Matthew, Thomas, and the rest.

Jesus didn't brag about saving the world. He didn't scold those who would turn against Him. He washed their feet. Jesus set the example, and He taught those who were chasing happiness to stop and consider what He did.

Finding and doing what God created you to do will bring more joy than you can imagine. But success and visible impact will tempt you to be proud. Pride, like many physical diseases, comes without warning. You can't see it or feel it, but it will slowly destroy you. Nothing destroys your joy like doing what God called you to do for the wrong reasons.

My father taught me that there are two things that reveal a person's character: money and power. I would add *influence* to his list. Knowing you can influence people and their decisions can inflate your ego. It gives you a false sense of importance. Success and influence affect our view of ourselves. Satan starts whispering in our ears, telling us how smart and how good we are, all while trying to get us to be like him instead of like Jesus.

The antidote to Satan's scheme is being a servant. It will keep you humble because only humble people can be servants. Proud people and insecure people want to be served instead of serving. Servants respect the thoughts and feelings of others. They are considerate and kind. They listen. That is why Paul instructed us, after giving Jesus as an example to follow, to "do all things without grumbling or

disputing" (Philippians 2:14). We grumble because we dislike someone or something. Grumbling is an outward sign of a selfish wish
that we could do or be somewhere different. Disputing or question-
ing is accusing others of an impure motive.

Paul expressed the importance of servanthood to the Romans
as well: "Love one another with brotherly affection. Outdo one
another in showing honor" (Romans 12:10).

After serving others, a servant has another goal: building others
up. The purpose of a servant is to make another person's life easier.
Sometimes it is a deed, such as babysitting for a single mom or keeping a special needs child so a couple can go to dinner. Other times,
it is running an errand for an elderly citizen or volunteering at the
library, tutoring a child, or mentoring a teenager.

Every servant knows his or her purpose. And servants look for
opportunities to fulfill that purpose by building people up as they
use the gifts God gave them.

Paul gave the Philippians two examples of true servants: Timothy
and Epaphroditus. Timothy's assignment from his Heavenly Father
was to assist Paul in his work. He was like Paul's own son (Philippians 2:22). But it was his humble servant's heart that encouraged
the Philippians. Timothy was "genuinely concerned" for their welfare (Philippians 2:20).

Epaphroditus knew his purpose was to do what was needed for
the church at Philippi and for Paul. He carried the letters from the
church to Paul and the letter from Paul to the church. As a servant,
Epaphroditus put the spiritual welfare of the church ahead of his
own physical health. In doing so, he nearly died (Philippians 2:30).

Paul wasn't advocating neglecting our health to help others, but he was stressing the willingness of a servant to serve. He was illustrating how people with a purpose, possessing a humble heart, get joy from helping people who need them.

> *Your security allows you to put others first.*

Personal Application

People without a purpose chase happiness because there is no satisfaction in just existing. There must be something more. A void of purpose creates a longing in the human heart. Insecure people think puffing themselves up, putting other people down, and trying to get ahead will give them what they desperately desire.

But it doesn't. Knowing that you were created to glorify God and that He has a special assignment for you gives you meaning and security—a security that allows you to put others first.

Read the second chapter of Philippians. Note how many times Paul used the word *humble* to describe Jesus. The sovereign God of the universe, living as a human body, was humble. Arrogance was not a characteristic of Jesus. Humility was.

Take a moment to think about these questions. Answer them honestly. Ask the Holy Spirit to help you see if your responses reveal a heart of pride or one of humility.

- Are you jealous when others succeed and you don't?
- Do you think people will accept you more if they know all the things you have accomplished?
- Are you happy if no one notices the things you do?
- How do you treat people who have nothing to offer in return?

When you find and live your purpose, you will discover joy in a new way. Be careful not to let pride rob you of that joy. Pride loves to chase happiness. Humility loves to help. So guard your heart.

Truth to REMEMBER

Humility is the most attractive part

of a person living with a purpose.

CHAPTER 7

Purpose Clarifies
YOUR PAST

*One thing I do: forgetting what lies behind
and straining forward to what lies ahead.*

Philippians 3:13

I will never forget his face.

He sat across from me in a booth at a restaurant. Earlier that evening, I spoke at a church he attended. The pastor asked me if I would be willing to talk with a young man after the service. Although I was tired, I agreed to meet him.

Drew was a young man in his early twenties, I

would guess. Well-dressed. Neat. Polite. And, based on his appearance, from a wealthy family. For several minutes, he sat staring at a cup of coffee. He found it difficult to look me in the eye.

Finally, he mumbled, "Phil, I can't believe what I've been through. I feel worthless. And to add to that, I've made some stupid decisions. I guess I've thrown my whole life away."

"Drew," I said, "I find that hard to believe. You are a young man. You have a lot of life yet to live." After a long pause, I continued by asking, "Why don't you start at the beginning?"

Over the next hour, Drew told me his story. It was obvious I wasn't the first to hear it, and this wasn't his first time to process the events of his life.

He was the oldest of three children. His family's wealth allowed him the best of everything. He wore only designer clothes. On his sixteenth birthday, he got a new Lexus. He was a successful athlete and a good-looking guy who could date any high school girl he wanted. And an honor student to boot. Drew graduated as the valedictorian of his large high school class and was offered academic scholarships to three Ivy League schools. To an outsider, life was good.

But inside, Drew was hurting. As a child, his uncle, who was highly respected in the community, started molesting him. He tried to tell his mother, but she refused to hear "another one of his lies."

He decided to attend Columbia University to study mathematics, with the dream of working in the space industry. His parents were proud. But back when Drew was in high school, he had begun to feel that he couldn't live up to his parents' expectations. He had tried, but the expectations were too high. Unknown to them, he had started drinking heavily and taking drugs he got from a friend. An addiction had quickly developed.

Drew was smart enough to be the head of his class but unable to deal with the addictions. Although his parents freely gave him money, he knew they would soon be suspicious. So to support his habit, he started stealing from his grandmother.

"Why didn't you ask for help?" I interjected.

"Because I was too proud and too embarrassed. And besides," he added, "when I was honest about the sexual abuse that I was experiencing, my mom didn't believe me. For her to acknowledge the abuse would mean that my mom's perfect world would be shattered. So, how do you think she would react if I told her that her son was a druggie?"

I knew he didn't want me to answer. I continued to listen.

One night, after a party with friends, Drew hit a car at an intersection, seriously wounding the driver. When the police arrived, Drew was too high to comprehend or explain what had happened. The police arrested him. He was charged with reckless endangerment.

At this point, Drew lifted his head and, for the first time, looked straight at me. He repeated something he heard at a youth camp when he was a teenager. He remembered a camp pastor saying, "The devil never charges you to enter his amusement park, but you pay a high price to get out."

This was his first arrest. He was a good student and had a family that could afford a good attorney. Drew was able to enter a plea bargain and avoid jail time. The judge gave him probation.

Drew's face bore the emotional scars of his past. The wrinkles denoted someone much older than he was. His eyes appeared hollow, telling everyone about the pain inside. I was uncertain what I needed to say. He was searching for encouragement or anything to give him hope. I did the best I could.

Years passed before I would see Drew again.

But when I did, his countenance was completely different. This time, there was a smile on his face, a precious wife and two kids by his side. His dream of working in the space industry had come true. That night, Drew asked if he could talk to me again. This time, he said it would be brief. We sat on the front row in the church auditorium.

"Phil, I want to thank you for what you said to me at the restaurant years ago. It radically changed my life," he said.

"That's wonderful! But so I can encourage others, what did I say?" I asked with a chuckle.

He told me with a smile that I said, "Drew, whatever you have done, whatever has been done to you, it does not change the purpose God created you for." Seeing Drew again made my day. I believed what I said then, and I believe it now:

> Regardless what has happened in your life…regardless of what your parents said about you or to you…regardless of what others did to you or what you did to yourself…God's mission and purpose for your life never changes!

The Past Shapes the Present

Drew's story gives us three lessons that illustrate how your past can affect you. Two are easy to see: the things people did to us, and the things we did. The third way isn't as obvious, as we will see later.

The Sins of Others

The sins and mistakes of the past are powerful emotional tools in the present. The sins others committed against you—especially abuse by a trusted adult or a spiritual leader—leave deep wounds that may require years of counseling. Maybe the betrayal of a spouse, a friend, or a business partner left you emotionally and financially ruined.

Sin hurts.

Suffering from the sins of others is one of the great mysteries that we can't fully grasp. It was that way from the beginning. The sin of Adam and Eve affected all of us. Death and pain entered the world by their disobedience. This is the first sin recorded in the Bible.

But did you know that the next sin after Adam and Eve's that is recorded in the Bible was when their son Cain killed their other son, Abel? Abel faithfully served God but suffered and died. Yet, Cain lived.

Throughout history, victims have suffered from the sins of others. King David is described as a man after God's own heart. God blessed his leadership, and Israel prospered. But David committed adultery with a woman named Bathsheba. A pregnancy resulted.

Bathsheba's husband, Uriah, was away fighting with the army. David sent for him, assuming that he would go home to his wife, and then everyone would assume the baby was his. Uriah, however, didn't visit his wife. So, to cover his sin, David instructed his military leader to put Uriah at the front of the army during the next conflict. As expected, Uriah died in the battle. When word reached the palace, David took Bathsheba as his wife. Uriah honored the Lord and his country. He did the right thing, but he died, and his wife went to live in the palace.

The wounds of sin are deep. Sometimes, sin harms the victim more than it hurts the perpetrator. And when the perpetrator doesn't even acknowledge the action or blames the victim, the pain deepens. If your past involves abuse and betrayal, it is natural to wonder, "Where was God? Why didn't He stop it? Didn't He care?"

God does care. We will have to wait until we get to heaven to understand why God allows innocent people to hurt because of the sins of others. But there is one thing I know: God can use the wounds in your past to magnify Him and fulfill the purpose He has for you.

Remember Joseph in the Old Testament? He was the favorite son of Jacob. To show his love, Jacob gave Joseph a special coat—a beautiful coat of many colors.

Joseph had a dream that revealed his purpose: He was born to be a leader of people. In his dream, Joseph saw a day when he would be a ruler, and his brothers would bow down to him. His older brothers already resented him; the dream only increased their hatred of him.

When Jacob sent Joseph to check on his brothers as they were tending sheep, they conspired to murder Joseph. One brother, Reuben, talked them out of killing him. Instead, they threw him in a deep pit. Not long after, a caravan of Ishmaelites came by on their way to Egypt. The brothers saw an opportunity and sold Joseph as a slave. Joseph was innocent, but the sins of his brothers put him into slavery.

The Ishmaelites, in turn, sold Joseph to Potiphar, an officer in Pharaoh's army. Potiphar saw Joseph's abilities and made him the overseer of his house. While a slave, Joseph's God-given purpose to lead others was beginning to make itself clear. The devil wasn't happy.

Joseph caught the attention of Potiphar's wife. She tried to get Joseph to have sex with her. He refused numerous times. It was wrong—a sin against God and against her husband. Joseph did the right thing, but Potiphar's wife later framed him by accusing him of trying to rape her. Potiphar believed his wife and sent Joseph to prison. Yet again, Joseph was innocent, but the sins of another put him behind bars.

Joseph continued to have a heart that honored God. In prison, he rose to be the respected leader among his fellow prisoners. Two prisoners from Pharaoh's kitchen—his cupbearer and his baker—were sent to the prison for making Pharaoh angry. Both prisoners had dreams that Joseph was able to interpret. In three days, he said, the cupbearer would be restored to his position, and the baker would be killed.

His interpretations came true.

Joseph's only request for the cupbearer when he was restored to his position was to speak favorably to Pharaoh about him. The cupbearer forgot. Joseph was faithful in serving God, but the lack of gratitude of another kept him in prison.

Two years later, when Pharaoh had a dream that no one could interpret, the cupbearer remembered Joseph's ability to interpret dreams. So Pharaoh sent for Joseph. Joseph explained that the dream meant there would be years of plenty followed by years of famine. Pharaoh believed him. To prepare for the coming famine, Pharaoh put Joseph in charge of planning for the anticipated food shortage.

Thousands of lives were saved by Joseph's foresight and planning, including the lives of Joseph's brothers and father. When his brothers came for grain, they bowed down to Joseph...just as he'd predicted they would when he was young. From the beginning, God's purpose for Joseph was to glorify God by helping others do things well. He was a gifted administrator. All the bad things that happened to Joseph would have destroyed him had he been focused on pursuing happiness. But his desire to fulfill the purpose God had for him caused him to rise above the hurt.

Joseph's life validates Romans 8:28: "We know that for those who love God all things work together for good, for those who are called according to his purpose." God turned Joseph's pain into preparation to fulfill his purpose. And God wants to turn your pain and your past into preparation for your purpose too.

People hurt people, but the pain differs from situation to situation. The pain you experienced may be so deep that you need a professional counselor to help you process it. If so, do it. Scripture doesn't forbid us from seeking help. Just like a medical doctor helps us heal physically, a counselor can help us heal emotionally and spiritually.

Scars are wounds that have healed. You will know the difference between a wound and a scar when you touch it. Wounds bring pain. Scars don't hurt. But if you refuse to nurse a wound, it will always be a wound.

Someday, your purpose may involve allowing people to see the mental scars others left in your life. Maybe not. But your scars will prove that wounds don't have to last forever.

> *God wants to turn your pain and your past into preparation for your purpose.*

Your Own Sin

Whether our past includes things done to us or by us, it affects who we are. It affects our emotions, how we view ourselves, and our interactions with others. It even affects our view of God.

Guilt is often associated with our conscience—our sense of right and wrong. But our natural conscience doesn't have a remedy for the past.

Jesus Christ does have a remedy for those who believe in Him.

For a Christian, it is important to separate the feelings of ongoing guilt from conviction by the Holy Spirit. The Holy Spirit's role is to make us aware of our sin, show us how wrong it is, and make us aware of its consequences. Jesus, in teaching His disciples about the Holy Spirit, said, "When he comes, he will convict the world concerning sin and righteousness and judgment" (John 16:8).

The Holy Spirit makes us aware so we can acknowledge our sin, turn from it, and accept the forgiveness of God.

But many people who repent still feel guilty and obsess over what they did wrong. Guilt makes them focus on their sin instead of on their Heavenly Father, who forgave them. The Bible uses three different word pictures to illustrate God's forgiveness.

First, the psalmist wrote, "As far as the east is from the west, so far does he remove our transgressions from us" (Psalm 103:12). Imagine you started traveling from east to west. Regardless of how long you traveled, or how far you went, you would always be headed west. That isn't true if you started traveling north. Eventually, you would be headed south. The word picture illustrates that when God forgives your sins, He throws them from His presence in a way that they can never return to Him.

The second word picture comes from an Old Testament prophet named Micah. He wrote, speaking of God, "You will cast all our sins into the depths of the sea" (Micah 7:19). That is, in a place where no one can see or find them. Corrie ten Boom said that God puts our sins in the deepest oceans and posts a sign that reads, "No Fishing Allowed!"

The third word picture is found in Isaiah 38:17. Isaiah wrote that our Heavenly Father has "cast all [our] sins behind his back." The area between your shoulder blades cannot be viewed by your eyes alone. Sure, you can see it in the reflection of a mirror, but without any aids, seeing the skin on your back is impossible. When God forgives, it is impossible for Him to see your sin again. So why are you staring at it? He never thinks about your forgiven sin, so why should you?

You are forgiven. Stop feeling guilty. If you don't, you will never fulfill the purpose God has for you.

Recognizing what we did that hurt others or ourselves may be easy to admit privately but hard to acknowledge publicly. Once you have confessed your sin to God and accepted His forgiveness, then ask God to give you wisdom to know what restitution, if any, you need to make.

One of the most memorable people Jesus met was Zacchaeus, a rich tax collector who lived in Jericho. Zacchaeus heard that Jesus was headed to his town. He wanted, more than anything, just to see this famous man.

Because he was short, seeing Jesus in a crowd was difficult. So, he ran ahead, climbed into a sycamore tree, and waited. As Jesus passed under the tree, He stopped, looked up at Zacchaeus, and told him to come down. And to the amazement of the crowd, Jesus announced that He was going to visit Zacchaeus's home.

As a tax collector for the Roman government, Zacchaeus had the power to charge more than the law required. That's how he became rich. Jews despised tax collectors, especially the dishonest ones. When Zacchaeus became a believer in Jesus, he addressed the wrongs that he had done to others. He immediately gave half of his wealth to the poor. And he announced that he would return four times any amount that he had taken dishonestly.

Returning what he stole wasn't a requirement for salvation or forgiveness. It did, however, demonstrate the sincerity of his repentance. After meeting Jesus, Zacchaeus wanted to live peacefully with his neighbors, but he also wanted to live with himself. Before we can pursue our purpose with passion, we must sometimes deal with the pain we caused others. Asking someone's forgiveness. Returning what we stole. Accepting responsibility for what we did. Publicly acknowledging our sin, especially when it affected our family, an organization, a community, or a church. All are things we may need to do to help us deal with the past.

Before we move on, we should discuss a feeling that's similar to but distinct from guilt: shame. Often the sin and abuse of another person that wounds us occurs when we are the least prepared to handle it. Joseph was a young boy when his brothers sold him into slavery. Children are often victims of sins just when they are learning to trust adults. And young Christians often face abuse by church leaders when they are first beginning to grow in their Christian lives. Even if it isn't a sin or abuse, the end of a relationship close to us hurts. How many times do children cry themselves to sleep because their mom and dad are getting a divorce? And because pain often comes when we are young, it is easy to assume that people abusing or misusing us is normal.

When we become young adults, we think that we are wise enough not to be betrayed or misused again. But then the one person we trusted and believed, the one person we swore would never betray us, does. The pain from being hurt sometimes causes us to turn the spotlight on ourselves. We often start to think that it was our fault. And when we do, shame fills our thoughts.

Shame is different from guilt.

Guilt is feeling bad about what you did. Shame is feeling bad about who you are.

Guilt says you made a mistake. Shame says you are a mistake.

Shame gets you to believe that the worst things said about you and to you are true. Shame whispers that no one likes you. Shame convinces you that you have no talents, no abilities, and no skills. Shame screams, "You are worthless!" And shame tries to make you believe that there is no reason to live.

But shame lies.

Shame is where the devil wants you to go mentally and emotionally. It keeps you hidden from the grace God wants to give. We don't know what to do with shame. Some try to numb it with alcohol or drugs. Others try to overcome it by being angry. And some try to ignore it. But Jesus wants to set you free from the lies you keep hearing.

On one occasion, Jesus met a large crowd after returning from a trip in a boat. A prominent man approached Jesus and pleaded for Him to come to his house and heal his 12-year-old daughter. Jesus agreed to go. As they were walking toward the man's house, a woman filled with shame approached Jesus from behind. For 12 years, she had a continual flow of blood that weakened her body. She spent everything she had going to doctors in hope of a cure.

But the problem she was experiencing went beyond the physical or financial. Jewish laws made her ceremonially unclean. That meant that no one could associate with her. She was forbidden to be near the temple area. She was physically, spiritually, financially, and socially shamed. For 12 years, the only conversations she'd been able to have were with other unclean people.

Shame kept her from seeking Jesus's help directly. But she knew that He had the power to heal her. She decided to approach Jesus from behind, touch the hem of the garment that He was wearing, and pray that no one would know. So, while the crowd pressed around Jesus, she touched Him. Immediately, her body was healed.

Jesus stopped. He asked, "Who touched me?" He knew, but more than healing her body, He wanted to heal her shame.

With fear, she admitted what she did. Jesus didn't shame her. He affirmed her by calling her "daughter"—a term that meant she was a clean daughter of Zion. No more hurting. No more hiding. She was free from shame!

Shame says that you will never have a purpose. Jesus says you are loved. Through fulfilling what He created you to be, you can live shame free.

Good Deeds

There is another way that our past becomes an obstacle to living our purpose. No one thinks of it as negative. In fact, most people applaud it. It is all the good things we have done. Things our community recognizes. Things that make our families proud. Even things that our churches commend.

In their rightful place, good deeds can be an asset to your purpose, which is often the direct result of doing them. But good, applaudable actions can keep you from what God designed you to be.

Shame reminds you of what others did to you. Guilt reminds you of what you did to yourself and to others. And pride keeps you from changing or doing what your Heavenly Father called you to do.

Paul knew it. He illustrated how easily it happens in the opening verses of the third chapter of Philippians. In the earliest days of the church, there was a group of devout Jews who believed that Jesus was the Messiah. They saw themselves as Christians. Most historians call them Judaizers. Judaizers taught that a Gentile had to become a Jew before he or she could become a Christian. For men, that meant they had to be circumcised. For men and women, it meant they had to keep Jewish rituals and ceremonies.

This group liked to go to areas where Paul and his associates had established a church and spread their teachings. Philippi was no exception.

Anyone who added requirements to grace angered Paul. That is why he called the Judaizers dogs, evildoers, and mutilators of the flesh. In using these words, Paul took the slang terms that devout Jews used to refer to Gentiles and used them to describe the Judaizers. The Judaizers could not accept that God wasn't impressed with their morality. So Paul described what a wonderful guy he was before God set him free from his religious past. Compared to them, Paul was the best of the best. He listed a number of areas where he was superior to them in their line of thinking.

- He was "circumcised on the eighth day," just as the Law required.
- The apostle was "of the people of Israel." That is, he was a full-blooded Jew.
- He was "of the tribe of Benjamin." Jews loved their ancestry, and every good Jew could trace their genealogy to one of the original 12 tribes of Israel. Next to Joseph,

Benjamin was Jacob's favorite son. And the tribe of Benjamin was only one of two (Judah being the other one) that remained faithful to the House of David. The other tribes refused to recognize a descendant of David as the heir to the throne.

- And Paul was a "Hebrew of the Hebrews." He wasn't just a good Jew from a Jewish family, but his family was devout. They rejected the lifestyles of the Greeks and Romans, probably spoke Aramaic in their home, and strictly adhered to the Law.

- Paul inherited all that, not to mention his family sending him to study under Gamaliel, the top Jewish expert and teacher in Jerusalem.

- Regarding choices he made as an adult, Paul was a passionate, committed Pharisee. Pharisees were the strictest group within the Jewish community.

Paul could brag. But he didn't. God had to strike Paul down with a bright light and speak audibly to get his attention. To fulfill his purpose in following Christ, Paul had to let go of his past too.

Anything negative from our past, we try to erase from our minds. It is painful, and we don't like pain. To dwell on it allows shame and guilt to grow. Positive stories from our past, on the other hand, give us a sense of security and well-being. They make us feel good, and we like to feel good. But if you think about the positive too much, it feeds your pride. And pride likes to chase happy. Pride causes you to avoid living by faith. If you are going to fulfill your divine purpose, faith is necessary.

Whether our past is good or bad or a mixture of the two, we must give it to our Heavenly Father and allow Him to use it for His glory and to enhance our purpose.

Prepared for a Purpose

A young couple asked if they could speak to me privately after one of the sessions at Celebrators—a conference our ministry conducts each fall. They attended with a group of older adults from their church.

They shared how they were certain God was calling them to be missionaries in a distant land. It was the reason, they believed, God created them and put them together. It was their purpose.

I was excited to hear the news. But then they started telling me all the reasons they couldn't do it. He was just honored as Teacher of the Year at the high school where he taught. She recently received a promotion where she worked. The boss told her that the primary reason for the promotion was the ethical standards she had—standards that he wanted other employees to follow.

Great jobs. Jobs with influence. Jobs with security. Good things, but not what God wanted them to do. Being a teacher or a business executive were their careers. Being missionaries was their purpose. For some, their purpose is teaching and impacting the lives of students. For others, it is being a Christian example in a secular place. But for this young couple, it wasn't.

Your present employment could be preparing you for your purpose, but it may not be God's purpose for your life. Teaching probably prepared the young man to teach on the mission field. And the business experience prepared the young lady for the business aspects of being a missionary. The question was, Could they let go of the good to do what God was telling them to do? Letting go of the good to fulfill their mission was hard. But the quiet, inner voice of the Holy Spirit kept reminding them what they were doing wasn't their purpose.

Personal Application

Regardless of your past, there is one thing to remember: God never wastes experiences, and He never wastes time. Whatever is in your past, God can use it if you give it to Him.

Find a quiet place and read the third chapter of Philippians, reflecting on the time and work Paul put into being a devout Jew. Paul called all the good he did to make himself acceptable to God "rubbish" or waste (Philippians 3:8). It was only when Paul realized that he was trying to earn God's favor—a favor that comes only through a relationship with Jesus Christ—that his past became an asset and not a liability. God didn't waste the experiences of Paul. God used him as a powerful preacher to help other Jews see Christ as the Messiah. And God used his education and persuasive skills to reach Gentiles as well.

But Paul also had some negative experiences in his past. He had to face the family members of Christians he persecuted and killed before he became a believer. What did he say when he saw them? How did they react? We don't know. But I sense that Paul sought their forgiveness and did everything that he could to help them.

Whatever your past holds, take time to meditate on the words of

Joseph to his brothers when they discovered his position in Egypt: "As for you, you meant evil against me, but God meant it for good, to bring it about that many people should be kept alive, as they are today" (Genesis 50:20).

Truth to REMEMBER

To fulfill your purpose, you must

stop living in the past. Give it to

God and start moving forward.

CHAPTER 8

Purpose Gives You GOALS

*I press on toward the goal for the prize
of the upward call of God in Christ Jesus.*

Philippians 3:14

can't believe it!"

That was my thought as I walked into a church auditorium where I was to speak moments later. Seated near the back of the room was an old friend—someone who was one of my best buddies when I was in my early twenties. Even though our lives had intersected a few times since then, this was the first time that I had seen him or talked with him in about 15 years.

Sitting in a restaurant later, we said to each other several times, "It's so great to see you!"

As we waited for our food, we took time to fill in the blanks for the years we had been apart. We talked about our kids and our grandchildren. It was encouraging to know that, for him, life was good.

Butch and I first met after we worked in a youth camp together. Late at night, sitting outside a cabin, we shared our dreams and our hopes. And we prayed together, asking our Heavenly Father to help us be faithful and godly men.

I already knew by our first meeting that God was calling me to preach, to write books, and to lead conferences to help people grow in their relationship with Jesus Christ. By my twentieth birthday, I had an organization to fulfill that purpose and was aggressively moving forward to make it happen.

Likewise, sitting outside that cabin, Butch shared the purpose our Heavenly Father had for him. He knew God wanted him to open a home for troubled boys. Not just another home, but one where they matched the personality types and personal skills of each boy with a career. He intended to get business leaders in that field to mentor each boy and, hopefully, by the time they were adults, they would be godly business leaders.

When we were in our midforties, our paths crossed again. Butch reaffirmed his purpose but hadn't started the home. It was, he emphasized, just a matter of time.

Now nearly 60, Butch shared his vision again as we ate. He was as clear and as passionate as he was 40 years ago. I was excited for him. "Butch, that's great! So, tell me about the home. Where is it? How many young men have been through the home?" I waited with anxious anticipation for his response.

Butch looked at me, no smile on his face.

Silence.

Then, in a shy, embarrassed voice, Butch said, "Well, we haven't started it yet. But we will one day soon."

Later that afternoon, I reflected on Butch and our conversation. Several times, he referred to the boys' home as his dream, his vision, and his purpose. It was genuine and heartfelt. But still unbuilt. I doubt Butch will ever live his purpose. For 40 years, he has been unwilling to take the first step, making excuses every time he needed to start.

Like a person wanting to learn how to swim but refusing to enter the water, or a person wanting to skydive but unwilling to get into the airplane, Butch will probably die knowing his purpose but never fulfilling it.

How Goals Lead to Action

Although I am in the ministry, my undergraduate degree is not in theology. My major was business administration. Or, to be more precise, administrative sciences. I was blessed to learn from some of the brightest and most insightful professors. They didn't just deal with theories but included the practical application of business principles. I learned how to write a business plan, read a financial report, and communicate clearly. Communication, I was taught, will take you where knowledge never can. Many people have great ideas, but they can't express their ideas in a way that others can understand.

And I was exposed to some of the prominent business leaders in America—men and women who have succeeded in the business world. They shared their secrets and the mistakes they had learned from. Every successful business leader I heard or read about in those days seemed to have two common traits: They all set goals, and they took steps to move forward.

One business leader whose work I read was Jim Rohn. Jim grew up on a farm and later worked for Sears. His skills landed him jobs with several multilevel marketing companies. Later, he became one of the top motivational speakers and consultants for major corporations. When he died in 2009 at the age of 79, the value of his estate was estimated at $500 million.

Of all the comments that I read by him, there is one that sticks in my mind. He said, "What separates the successful from the unsuccessful so many times is that the successful simply do it. They take action."

He was right. If I summarized everything I learned about business at the University of Alabama, I would summarize it this way: Goals determine actions, actions express your priorities, and priorities demonstrate what you are trying to achieve.

And I would add that your priorities should be determined by your purpose. In fact, for the Christian, I think these steps should be arranged in reverse order. Find your purpose, and set your priorities by it. Let your priorities determine your actions. And put your actions in place by setting goals.

> *Your priorities should be determined by your purpose.*

Jesus passed through Samaria on His way from Judea back to Galilee. Devout Jews avoided Samaria like it was a land infested with a plague. They viewed Samaritans as half-breeds who were unworthy of God's love.

Jesus was tired and thirsty from the journey. He sat down by Jacob's well. The well was deep, and He had nothing to use to draw water. So He waited.

Finally, a woman came to get water, and Jesus asked her for a drink. His request shocked the woman. "How is it that you, a Jew, ask for a drink from me, a woman of Samaria?" (John 4:9).

Jesus explained that if the woman understood who He was, she would ask *Him* for a drink, and He would give her living water. Those who drank the water He offered would never thirst again. In fact, Jesus said that the living water would become in her "a spring of water welling up to eternal life" (John 4:14).

It is interesting to know how this woman chased happiness all her life and found it meaningless. Happiness, she thought, was found in various relationships with men. Jesus revealed that she had been through five marriages and was living with a man who was not her husband. She longed for love and joy in her heart—something no man or woman could give her. Only Jesus could do that.

Individuals have always chased happiness in different ways. Some look for it in relationships, others in their careers. Some worked to be the best in a sport, only to find no lasting satisfaction. From movie stars to local bankers, from social media experts to work-from-home moms, many have reached the top of their professions only to find loneliness. Sadly, many have taken their own lives, convinced that life has no meaning. All these people have looked for meaning in a place they would never find it.

The woman at the well had a choice: *Do I continue to do it my way? Or do I put my trust in a man who told me everything?* She acted on faith. She chose Jesus.

The Joy That Brings Meaning

The apostle Paul understood that the greatest inclination for Christians is to assume that their lives will be filled with meaning once they have trusted Christ. Granted, that is the first step toward finding meaning in this present life, but there is more that believers must do to find the joy they desperately desire.

The book of Philippians is called the joy epistle. Even a casual reader can detect that Paul is helping believers at Philippi experience real joy. And, for Paul, *joy* is the word that best describes a life lived with a mission and a purpose. It is obvious that Paul is experiencing the joy he describes—a joy that gives life meaning and makes every day worth living.

And remember, Paul isn't writing from a mansion surrounded by servants. He is writing from a prison surrounded by soldiers. Unlike most famous celebrities, Paul had joy regardless of what was happening around him. In the third chapter of Philippians, he shared his secrets.

Focus on Your Mission

Activity for its own sake is worthless. Imagine a person who gets in their car and drives around town without a destination. Later, they can report that they drove, burned fuel, and put miles on their vehicle, but they accomplished nothing.

Before you set out to fulfill your purpose, make sure you keep the mission in mind. Ask, "Why am I doing this?" That is because one of the greatest temptations believers face is focusing so much on their purpose that they forget the reason behind it. Their "what" begins to obscure the "why."

In the third chapter of Philippians, after Paul issued his challenge to the Judaizers who taught that becoming a Jew was a prerequisite to being a Christian, he wrote about his own personal relationship with Christ. He explained the mission of glorifying God in greater detail. The motive behind glorifying God is "that I may know him and the power of his resurrection, and may share his sufferings, becoming like him in his death, that by any means possible I may attain the resurrection from the dead" (Philippians 3:10-11).

In other words, our mission is to become more like Jesus every day. Our thoughts, our attitudes, and our actions should reflect our desire to magnify our Heavenly Father in every area of our lives.

Set Your Priorities

If you are going to carry out your purpose, it will force you to put your priorities in order. You must determine what is most important and what is not. You will have to decide what you need to start doing, what you need to continue doing, and what you need to stop doing. And you need to learn to say "no," even to good things.

On a trip to New England a few years ago, I decided to visit the home of Dwight L. Moody. Moody was a great evangelist in the late nineteenth century. His crusades drew great crowds and brought many people to Christ. Moody lived in Northfield, Massachusetts. The home where he was born and the house where he died stand close together. He and his wife are buried behind his birthplace.

Stored in his birthplace are several Bibles that Moody used in his lifetime. In many of these, he wrote notes or slogans that he heard, probably to use while preaching. In one of the Bibles I picked up, Moody had written, "Every cause is not a call."

I don't know when Moody wrote those words or why. It may have been shortly after the Great Chicago Fire in October 1871. Moody preached in Chicago the night the fire began. Many of the people who heard Moody preach weren't Christians, and they didn't respond that night. As a result, Moody realized the urgency of sharing the gospel and bringing people to a life with Christ.

Before the fire, Moody was involved in many different projects—good ones, like the YMCA, Sunday school promotion, and publishing. But after the fire, Moody rearranged his priorities and focused on what he believed was his purpose in life: preaching in mass meetings and pleading for unbelievers to trust Christ.

When I read Moody's comment, I, too, changed my priorities.

If you want to know your priorities—not what you say they are, but what they really are—there are two ways to find out: Look at your bank account, and examine your schedule. How you spend your money and your time reflect your true priorities.

Paul set an example by putting his purpose first and everything else after it. That is why he could write "one thing I do" (Philippians 3:13) when he described his walk with God. He was disciplined about his priorities.

Get Started

When I think about my friend Butch, I sincerely believe that he wants to magnify God in his life. He loves Jesus, and his character reflects it. But he keeps waiting to start fulfilling his God-given assignment in life.

When I asked him why he waited, he gave me a list of reasons—good reasons in his mind. But I call them excuses. Before you start fulfilling your purpose, there will always be a reason to procrastinate.

My wife, Debbie, and I enjoy taking trips, often to the mountains of Tennessee and the beaches of northwest Florida. We drive to both destinations. And in a five- or six-hour trip, we will encounter lots of red lights. Suppose we thought about all the red lights before we left home? And what if we waited until all the lights turned green to depart? Then we would never leave home.

Nothing worth doing is without obstacles. I often remind myself what Henry Ford, the famous automaker, said about challenges you will face: "Obstacles are those frightening things you see when you take your eyes off the goal."

Instead of waiting for everything to be perfect, Butch could have been researching the various laws affecting a home for boys. He could have shared his vision with potential donors. And he could have met with others who ran similar homes about the challenges he would face. But he didn't. He kept waiting. And that is why, I believe, he will never experience the joy that God intends for him to have.

Ignore the Distraction

Paul was a man of action. He didn't make excuses, but he knew that it was hard to stay focused on magnifying God in our lives and keeping the right priorities. There would be distractions.

Distractions come from three places: behind you, around you, and in front of you.

Behind you. Behind you is your past. Not just the bad things that were done to you or by you, but the simple mistakes you make—things that make you feel dumb.

I remember meeting an elderly lady who told me that she only drove a vehicle once. I asked her, "Why just once?"

"Well," she said, "my husband wanted me to learn how to drive. He drove our 1951 pickup into our pasture. I got in the driver's seat and did what he told me to do."

"And?"

"Well, I misunderstood and kept pressing the gas when I should have pressed the brake. I drove it into the fence, and I decided then and there that I would never drive again," she said with a chuckle.

It may not have been while driving, but all of us have had similar experiences. Something happened. We were embarrassed, felt like a fool, and determined then and there never to do it again.

Don't let past mistakes keep you from trying again. When you find your purpose and act on it, you will make lots of mistakes. Learn from them, but don't let them keep you from advancing in your purpose.

Around you. Around you are critics—people like the Judaizers were to Paul—who try to undermine everything you do. Most of them aren't fulfilling their purpose, and you are intimidating them. Don't listen to them. Keep working.

In the Old Testament, Nehemiah was a Jew who was in captivity in Babylon. He heard about the condition of Jerusalem, how the walls were destroyed. Nehemiah sought and received permission from the king of Babylon to return and restore the walls. When he did, two men became his harshest critics: Sanballat and Tobiah. They criticized Nehemiah. They tried to undermine his credibility, and even tried to attack him and his workers.

But Nehemiah never allowed his critics to get the best of him. He kept working, fulfilling his purpose. When his critics wanted to meet with him to "do me harm," Nehemiah responded, "I am doing a great work and I cannot come down. Why should the work stop while I leave it and come down to you?" (Nehemiah 6:3).

In front of you. Then, there is the future.

If I had known in 1980, when our ministry was just getting started, everything I would face in the coming decades, I would have been trembling. Fear would have emotionally paralyzed me. I knew what I was called to do, but I didn't see the extent of the responsibility that came with the ministry.

That is why the future involves faith. Our Lord isn't going to show you everything about the road ahead or how He is going to use you. Nor will He show you where you will go or whom you will touch.

Don't fret about what is behind you, ahead of you, or around you. Just ask God to keep you focused whenever a distraction comes along. Be like Paul: "Forgetting what lies behind and straining forward to what lies ahead, I press on" (Philippians 3:13-14).

Set Goals

Any business leader knows goal-setting is essential to success. And setting goals can be a big asset to your Christian life and living your purpose.

Goals are not wishes or dreams. They are measurable achievements to keep us focused and disciplined. Paul expressed his main goal in Philippians 3:14. He wrote, "I press on toward the goal for the prize of the upward call of God in Christ Jesus."

At first glance, you may think Paul was restating his mission to glorify God. In a sense, he was. But when you understand the image Paul had in mind, you see the big goal of his life was the culmination of a set of smaller goals that he wanted to achieve.

In Paul's day, Olympic-style games were the sporting events of the year. They involved sports such as running, chariot races, boxing, gladiator fights, and various forms of ball games.

And winning was a big deal. Like today, athletes trained to be the best. They exercised daily, watched their diet, and trained with other competitors in the sport. Their goal was to win the prize. This prize was usually a wreath worn as a chaplet around the head or as a garland around the neck. The winner was called to a platform in front of the crowd to receive the prize, usually from the emperor.

Paul knew that one day he would stand before God to receive rewards for his faithful service. He wanted to do everything God purposed for him to do so that he might receive a reward, or "prize." But to receive that prize, Paul had smaller goals to help him achieve that one. He planned his missionary journeys carefully. The apostle looked for opportunities to preach, and intentionally started churches in places where God called him.

Paul didn't wait around, hoping something would happen. He planned. He worked. And he set goals—goals that aligned with the ultimate goal of being faithful in his purpose.

If you are going to achieve your purpose, you must set goals and deadlines. Sure, situations may warrant that they be modified along the way. Without goals, you will be like my friend Butch, always dreaming but never achieving.

Choose Your Mentors Wisely

Paul gave the Philippians a strong warning: "Brothers, join in imitating me, and keep your eyes on those who walk according to the example you have in us" (Philippians 3:17). And he added that people with wrong motives will lead you astray.

The main characteristic of a person seeking to serve our Lord is a teachable spirit. Regardless of what God has for you to do, you need others to speak into your life. But choose those people wisely.

First, they should be godly people who are committed to the mission of glorifying God and carrying out their purpose in His plan. That doesn't mean that we cannot learn from unbelievers or ungodly people, but we must listen to their words with discernment. If their counsel contradicts the teachings of Scripture or tries to get us to do something the Bible calls unwise, avoid them at all costs.

And they should have your best interest in mind. Many Christians want to live their purpose through you. Maybe they know their assignment from the Lord is like yours. Maybe they have a good motive, but they would feel better about their failure to do what God told them to do if you failed as well.

Your mentors should be people you choose, not people who volunteer to help. Too many people want to control other Christians by appearing to help but are trying to extend their own power.

Stay Strong

If Paul can be open and honest, I should be too.

After being in ministry 40 years, doing what God designed and called me to do, the challenge isn't getting started. I did that.

It isn't having the right advisers. I've done that.

My challenge is growing weary in the work. It is staying excited and motivated. It is setting new goals that require a step of faith.

How many Christians have I met who found their purpose and started living it, only to be discouraged and quit? Too many. Most thought they could maintain their joy, but they lost it too. Encouragement and accountability are essential. Without them, you will start assuming the Lord's blessings will always be present. You will procrastinate. Before long, you will cease magnifying God in your life.

Maybe that is why Paul's last word in this section on straining toward the goal is summarized as, "My brothers, whom I love and long for, my joy and crown, stand firm thus in the Lord, my beloved" (Philippians 4:1).

> *Knowing your purpose doesn't prompt joy to flood your emotions. Acting on your purpose does.*

Personal Application

Finding your purpose is the first step in living a life filled with joy. But knowing your purpose doesn't prompt joy to flood your emotions. Acting on your purpose does.

One thing that keeps me on track is a journal. I have my mission statement for my life written in it where I can see it every day. I have my goals listed there, as well as the practical ways that I will fulfill them. And I keep a daily record of my thoughts, fears, and emotions. I note how the Lord is working in my life—what He is teaching me and how. I write down my mistakes as well as my blessings.

Keeping a journal helps me do two things. First, it forces me to think through what I am feeling and what I am experiencing. And second, it allows me to look back through the past years to see how God has worked in my life and ministry.

A journal is for oneself, not others. Some things are so personal that they never should be shared. In those cases, I write my thoughts and feelings on a separate piece of paper and then shred it. In my journal, I may make notations of which I alone know the meaning. But when it comes to the day-to-day lived experience of faith and action, a journal is a great way to see how you are progressing on your goals. It helps you see how far you have come and how far you have to go.

Truth to
REMEMBER

You will never know joy if you

keep putting your purpose in a file

marked "One of These Days." Start

fulfilling it today, even if the first step

is a small one. Take the next one

tomorrow, and keep moving forward.

CHAPTER 9

Purpose Values
RELATIONSHIPS

*Do nothing from selfish ambition or conceit, but
in humility count others more significant than
yourselves. Let each of you look not only to his
own interests, but also to the interests of others.*

Philippians 2:3-4

You have watched it happen many times.

Two people, inseparable best friends, suddenly have a rift. One refuses to speak to the other. Her friend responds by thinking, "Fine. If that's the way she wants it, so be it."

Times passes. Each one is waiting for the other one to make a move, to apologize so the friendship can be restored. Nothing happens because pride prevents it.

Two friends, two family members, two business associates who thought nothing or anyone could come between them. A relationship that took them through hard times and good times together. They laughed together on vacation and cried together at family funerals. Two friends shared their deepest frustrations and their greatest joys. They shared secrets and dreams. Then, one misunderstanding or unkind word ended it all.

It has happened to others. It happened to me. And it probably has happened to you.

You might think that conflict only happens to unbelievers—people who have no faith in Jesus Christ. Think again. It happens to Christians too. Churches split. Members leave one church and join another. Believers who once called each other brothers and sisters in Christ resolve never to speak to each other again; that is, unless the other person admits he or she was wrong, amends their ways, and publicly tells everyone how foolish they were for acting the way they did.

Everyone needs relationships. We need people to love, and we need people to love us. You need people to encourage, and you need people to encourage you. Our Lord never intended for people to live the Christian life alone. If He did, all of us would have our own private island somewhere in the South Pacific. And if God intends for individuals to be in our lives, then other people are essential to accomplishing our purpose.

We need people. We need people to pour into our lives, and we need to pour into the lives of others. If we don't, isolation occurs. And isolation is a fertile territory for temptation and sin.

That is why the apostle Paul, writing to the church at Philippi, paused in his letter to write a brief note to two women in the church, Euodia and Syntyche. Apparently, these two women had a disagreement, probably about something in the church.

Did Syntyche say something that hurt Euodia's feelings? Did Euodia neglect one of Syntyche's children in a Christmas program? Was it a political issue? Was one trying to control the other?

Honestly, we don't know. Paul said these two women were believers. In fact, Paul affirmed their salvation as genuine when he said that their names were written in the book of life (Philippians 4:3). The book of life was a reference to people saved by grace and assured of a home in heaven. Paul added that the two women worked with him and other church leaders to reach those who didn't know Christ. The two women not only worked with others, they worked together. There was a time when they encouraged and supported each other.

It is possible these two women had a long friendship. When Paul and Silas first arrived in Philippi, they met a group of ladies praying by the river. And from that prayer meeting, God began to move in the city. Lydia was the only woman mentioned by name at the meeting, but Euodia and Syntyche may have been present.

If Euodia and Syntyche refused to reconcile and value their relationship, they would lack joy. So Paul appealed to each woman personally to "agree in the Lord" (Philippians 4:2). He didn't prefer one over the other, nor did he say who was right and who was wrong.

Paul wanted them to see how much they needed each other—for their sake and for the sake of the church. Fulfilling their purpose in the kingdom of God required it.

Satan works hard to destroy relationships, especially among Christians. He knows how powerful healthy relationships can be in helping you live God's purpose for your life. The devil will try to destroy your marriage, to put distance between you and your children, and even try to put wedges between you and other family members. Satan delights in causing divisions between believers. He knows that broken relationships weaken a church's effectiveness, leaving the message of the gospel tainted in a community.

Broken relationships keep you from your purpose. We must guard our hearts from feelings and thoughts that harm and destroy how we value people.

> *Other people are essential to accomplishing our purpose.*

Comparison

We like to compare ourselves to others to see how we are doing, as a way of measuring up. Perhaps we compare ourselves to see who's the most attractive, who's the richest, who's the most athletic, who's the most successful in their career.

But comparison ruins you. It demolishes your passion and your motivation. It kills your confidence and self-worth. It robs you of your inner peace and steals your contentment. No matter where you look, if you compare yourself to others, you will always find someone smarter, richer, and more attractive. There is always someone more successful, more effective, and better liked.

Maybe that is why Paul, writing earlier in Philippians, limited his comparisons to his earlier self and Jesus. That was a healthy comparison because it allowed Paul to see if he was progressing or digressing in his spiritual life. This is a healthy exercise for us to do as well.

But the real standard for comparison is Jesus. How do we compare to Him? Are we becoming every day a little more like Him?

Comparing yourself to others will make you bitter. Comparing yourself to Jesus will make you better.

Arrogance

Comparing yourself to others often prompts you to feel inferior. But more damage is done when it causes you to feel superior.

People will rarely admit they feel superior, but they'll reveal their attitude in their words. They easily find a reason why others aren't up to their standards. "Those people" are lazy, dumb, uneducated, or socially challenged. Or they lack motivation.

Perhaps you don't think you fall into the "feeling superior" category. But when is the last time you hugged a homeless person, interacted with a mentally ill person, or mentored a low-income child? Aren't these people valuable to God?

Jesus was once talking with a group of people who felt superior to others. The Bible called them a group of people "who trusted in themselves that they were righteous, and treated others with contempt"

(Luke 18:9). The story was about two men—a Pharisee and a tax collector—who went to pray. The Pharisee, feeling superior, thanked God that he wasn't like other people, especially the tax collector. And he reminded God of his faithfulness to fast and pay his tithes.

The tax collector, though, compared himself to God's standard, not the standard of his own goodness, causing him to see himself as a sinner. He pleaded for God to be merciful to him. Jesus affirmed that the tax collector, not the Pharisee, was justified in the eyes of God.

If you value people as God values them, you won't feel superior. And who knows? You may find your purpose among the people you have avoided.

Jealousy

For most of us, feelings of inferiority control our thoughts. We look at others and desire what they have. Maybe it is their looks, their job, their relationships, or their stuff. We can't see what we have because we are so fixated on what they have.

King Saul, the first king of Israel, led his troops to fight the Philistines. The Philistines had a secret weapon: a giant named Goliath. Goliath stood over nine feet tall! He challenged any one man to single combat. The winner would be declared the victor of the battle, with the losing army surrendering.

Saul wasn't just the king but also the tallest man in the army. It was logical that he would be the one to fight Goliath. But he refused, fearing that he would be defeated.

David, who came to see his brothers, stepped forward to fight the giant. With one stone in his slingshot, he killed Goliath. Israel won.

But the people started praising David. Saul grew jealous. Saul learned that Samuel had anointed David to be the next king. Instead of honoring God, Saul vowed to kill David. Saul hated David till the day he died.

Jealousy will destroy a marriage, a career, a church, and a friendship. Jealousy keeps you from seeing and admitting the truth. It keeps you from having healthy relationships.

Envy

Jealousy doesn't stop at making us feel worse about ourselves. It invites envy to live in our hearts with it.

Anyone with teenagers in their home can testify to the power of envy. If a new girl comes to a school, and she suddenly catches the attention of the most popular guy in the school, all the girls join together to exclude her from their group. Girls hold parties and intentionally make sure the new girl isn't invited...and they make sure she knows it.

But it isn't just girls. Envy affects boys too. Boys take verbal jabs at someone getting more attention by making fun of any embarrassing information they can find. When the person makes a mistake, they make sure everyone knows about it.

Then, teenagers grow up. And they bring their envy with them into adulthood.

Envy is secretly wishing you were someone else. You feel entitled to more than what you have. Envy makes you look at God and say, "It's not fair!"

There are two sisters in the Old Testament that demonstrate

the destructive hold that envy can have on us. Their names were Leah and Rachel. Both women were married to Jacob. Jacob, at first, wanted to marry Rachel, and he worked for her father seven years to win her hand in marriage. But when the wedding day came, Rachel's father tricked him, and Jacob married Leah instead. Jacob then worked another seven years to get to marry Rachel.

Two women married to the same man. And both of them envied the other. Leah was able to have children, and Rachel wasn't. Rachel envied Leah's ability to have children, causing her to resent God and her sister. But Leah was envious of Rachel because she was Jacob's first love.

Leah wanted to be loved. Rachel wanted to have children. Neither could see the blessings they had because they were too focused on what they didn't have.

Envy despises someone's attractiveness and popularity. And envy resents what someone is able to do that you can't. Envy causes you to think the purpose God gave someone else is better than the role He gave you. When we think this way, life loses its meaning, and joy departs.

That is why Solomon wrote, "A tranquil heart gives life to the flesh, but envy makes the bones rot" (Proverbs 14:30). Envy sucks the life right out of you.

Gossip

Jesus said that what is in your heart will come out of your mouth. Jealousy and envy are no exceptions.

We confidentially share with people negative information about mutual acquaintances. We want to keep people from thinking more highly of them than of us. Gossip is the words uttered from a heart filled with jealousy and envy. Gossip reveals our insecurity. It reveals a desperate need for attention or importance.

People who gossip are trying to be special, elevating themselves by exposing a secret or a negative opinion of someone. And their motive is often to get someone to tell them their secrets and opinions so they can go share the gossip with others. Gossip reveals more about the person sharing the information than about the listeners because people who gossip are lonely, insecure, and immature.

Former First Lady Eleanor Roosevelt is quoted as saying, "Great minds discuss ideas. Average people discuss events. Small minds discuss people." According to Revelation 12:10, Satan loves to spread gossip. So, when you are gossiping, are you being like Jesus or the devil?

Like anyone else, I've been caught in the trap of gossip, both as the gossiper and the one who was the subject of the gossip. Neither is helpful. Both are hurtful.

There are two things I've discovered. First, people who gossip with you will gossip to others *about* you. Second, it is very difficult to gossip about anyone you pray for.

One final thought about gossip. If people are coming to you sharing gossip, there is probably a good reason. You are listening to it and encouraging them to share it. When people need a place to put garbage, they start looking for a garbage can. If people are sharing their garbage with you, stop it. You are not a garbage can.

Maybe the best advice I've received about gossip came from an elderly preacher from my childhood. He often said, "There is so much bad in the best of us, and so much good in the worst of us, that it behooves all of us to stop talking about the rest of us."

Healthy Relationships

Some relationships are difficult to navigate because people will lash out and hurt us in an effort to control us or a situation. Often, we need to remember that difficult people are usually people who have been hurt. They are like an injured animal; you try to help but get bit in the process. Hurting people wound the one who is trying to relieve their pain.

Fortunately, most of our relationships, whether casual or close, have the potential to be healthy and whole. In all of these situations, we need to value people because God created them, remembering He loves them as much as He loves us. Yes, relationships can be challenging. Sometimes we have to set boundaries to protect us or the other person. But don't let the challenging relationships keep you from having healthy ones.

Healthy relationships are rare. But they are healthy because each person is intentional in having a wholesome companionship. Here are a few characteristics of a healthy relationship.

Acceptance

Relationships are challenging because real relationships make us vulnerable. They involve risk, but the risk is worth it. It is impossible to magnify God and find your purpose if you lack healthy relationships in your life. People need you, and you need people!

As young children, we felt rejection when someone said something negative about us or repeated a story about our foolish mistakes. Other children laughed at us, perhaps to prevent us from being someone's friend. Adults, trying to deal with their own struggles, say things to us and about us that make us feel flawed. So, we put a wall around our heart, thinking it will protect us from more pain and rejection.

But inside every human being is a longing to be accepted for who they are, not for the image they feel forced to project. Accepting doesn't mean approving someone's politics, opinions, or actions. Accepting is not affirming their beliefs or actions. Healthy relationships give each person the freedom to breathe, to be who they are, faults and failures included.

If you need a model of accepting people, look at Jesus. Religious leaders of His day thought that love was forcing everyone to look, act, and think like them. Jesus didn't approve of the sin of the woman caught in adultery, the crimes of the thief on the cross, or the self-righteousness of Nicodemus. And yet, He allowed children to be children, the outcast to touch Him, and those whom society rejected to eat with Him.

High Value

Shortly after Debbie and I married, we attended a weekend marriage seminar. The leader did an excellent job teaching about communication, making time for each other, and all the other issues that married couples face.

When we gathered for the Saturday morning session, as the speaker casually put his microphone on his lapel, he started talking to a young couple on the front row. His microphone was live, and everyone could hear what was being said.

He told the young couple that his ministry recently received a special gift. An elderly lady gave him a very expensive diamond. In fact, he said, it was appraised at two million dollars!

He then reached into his backpack and pulled out the diamond and showed it to them. The young couple was in awe.

When he looked up, the speaker realized we all were listening. Then, he asked if all of us would like to see the diamond. One or two verbalized a "yes," so he said he would pass it around. His only request was for us to be careful when we held it because dropping it could damage it and decrease its value.

When the diamond came to us, Debbie didn't want to touch it, fearing she might drop it. I carefully took it into my hand. It sparkled in the light. Then, I very carefully passed it to the man seated beside me, relieved I wasn't holding it any longer.

After the last person saw it, the speaker retrieved it and asked, "Were you all careful with it?"

"Yes," we assured him in unison.

Then, the speaker made an announcement: The stone wasn't a diamond but a piece of inexpensive cut glass. It was appraised by him at two million dollars, but on the open market it was worth about five dollars.

It was his concluding remark that I can't forget. "You handled this glass carefully because you believed it had value. And how you handle any relationship in your life is directly related to how much value you assign to it."

Treat people like they have high value. Your purpose demands it.

Listening

The greatest gift we can give in a relationship is listening. Good listeners are tuned in to what a person is saying, both with their words and their actions.

Good listeners don't look at their cell phone or glance at their watch. They don't give advice unless asked. And they don't unload their problems at the same time a friend is sharing their heart.

Everyone has different amounts of money, but everyone has the same amount of time. When you listen, you give people the gift of your time—a gift that they will treasure forever.

Encouragement

Closely associated with the gift of listening is the gift of your words—encouraging words that convey value. Encouragement is reminding people of the gifts and talents they possess and giving them the courage to use them. It is helping them live another day or face a problem.

When you encourage others, you are like a cheerleader for a sports team. You can't live their lives for them, just like a cheerleader can't make a play for the team. But you can let them know you believe in them, and they are going to make it.

Paul had an encourager. His name was Barnabas. He traveled with Paul on his early missionary trips. In fact, it was Barnabas who first believed Paul's account of his salvation experience on the

Damascus Road. Other Christians were doubtful, thinking it might be a trick to persecute them.

Paul and Barnabas once had a major disagreement. A young man named John Mark was an assistant on one of their journeys, but he quit and went home. When Paul and Barnabas were going to return to the mission sites, Barnabas wanted to take John Mark along, but Paul refused. Disagreeing, Barnabas took John Mark, and Paul took Silas, forming two teams to do missionary work.

But Paul valued Barnabas and John Mark, even if they disagreed. Paul's writings indicate that he worked with both of them again and placed a high premium on their relationship. The encouragement Barnabas gave Paul turned him into one of the great leaders of early Christianity. And the encouragement Barnabas gave John Mark also produced an early church leader—a man who wrote one of the four Gospels: the Gospel of Mark. Encouragement causes people to do things greater than they imagined.

By the way, the real name of Barnabas was Joseph. Barnabas was a nickname. It meant "son of encouragement" (Acts 4:36). To put it another way, he was so effective at encouraging people, they said he was encouragement's son—a very high compliment.

Service

Debbie and I have a friend who lived next door to a grumpy old man. No one liked him. When he came outside, it was to complain.

Knowing that love leads to action, our friend decided she and her family would look for ways to serve him. They brought his garbage can from the street to his house. They pulled the weeds from his flower bed. When he was sick, they mowed his lawn and drove him to the doctor. Learning he had no family, they started celebrating his birthday and took him gifts at Christmas. Every chance they had, they served him.

Slowly, the grumpy old man became a friend, often doing things for them in return.

Today, he is a Christian and a friend to all the neighbors. Instead of being grumpy, he smiles. All because some neighbors loved him by serving him.

Just like Jesus.

Personal Application

People can be the greatest source of joy in your life or the greatest source of pain. And painful relationships often keep us from the ones filled with joy.

Take an inventory of your relationships. Classify them as close, casual, or distant. Be sure to note the ones that moved from one category to another during the past few years.

Now evaluate them. Beside each name, note the last time you sincerely listened to that person. When was the last time you encouraged them? And when was the last time you served them?

Make another list. This time list people you know casually from church, your community, or work who don't appear to have many healthy relationships. Ask God to help you establish one so they might come to know Christ by your witness and grow in their relationship with the Lord.

And if you don't have many healthy relationships, take time to meditate on the wisdom of Solomon in Proverbs 18:24 (NKJV): "A man who has friends must himself be friendly."

Truth to REMEMBER

Relationships are as vital to your

purpose as air is to your lungs.

CHAPTER 10

Purpose Provides
CONTENTMENT

*I have learned in whatever
situation I am to be content.*

Philippians 4:11

finally found the life I've always wanted. Find
your purpose, and do it!"

Those words hung in the air. The audience sat
silently, as if waiting to hear them again. They were
the concluding words of an actor who, for the previous 45 minutes, portrayed the life of King Solomon
on stage.

Solomon was the son of King David. He was the last great king of a united Israel—a king known for his wisdom and wealth. You probably would think a person with absolute power, limitless money, and a brilliant mind would be the happiest person on earth. But he wasn't. In fact, Solomon was miserable.

When he was young, Solomon thought love was the secret to happiness. If he could marry the woman of his dreams, they would live happily ever after. Solomon met her. She was, in his opinion, the most beautiful woman in the world. But it didn't bring the happiness he thought it would.

So, he added another wife, then another, and yet another. In all, Solomon married over 700 women! Not to mention his 300 concubines. He had his pick of over 1,000 women, but happiness eluded him.

If women couldn't do it, Solomon thought wealth could. He amassed real estate holdings, building mansions on lakes surrounded by the finest gardens and parks. They were all staffed to make them immaculate and to provide any wish Solomon desired. But Solomon continued to be miserable.

Maybe, Solomon thought, we just aren't partying enough. His servants brought out wine and the best musicians in the land. And they partied until they could party no more. But Solomon was still miserable.

The king thought his misery came from his lack of productivity, so work became his priority. Yet Solomon remained miserable.

Nothing satisfied him. So finally, after he chased happiness harder and longer than anyone in history and spared no expense to do it, having depleted every possible source of happiness, Solomon concluded that chasing happiness was equivalent to chasing the wind. Only after exhausting every resource in the pursuit of happiness did Solomon discover the secret to a fulfilling life: Magnify God by finding your purpose and doing it.

What Solomon wanted to experience—what all of us want—is significance. We want to know our lives matter and feel secure about who we are. We want to know that we are making a difference. We want to be useful.

When Paul wrote the book of Philippians, his intent was to help the Christians in Philippi know the excitement that comes from being a part of God's plan for the world. But Paul didn't start his letter by telling them the benefits. He laid a foundation that focused on God. It isn't our plans. It is His. That's why the first three chapters of Philippians stressed the necessity of seeing life from God's viewpoint, making godly choices, being an unselfish role model, pursuing a goal, and valuing people. If you don't have a solid foundation for your actions, you won't apply what you hear, and you will miss the purpose for your life.

It is important to note that the feelings you desperately desire are not your target. Serving God is the focus. But your Heavenly Father gives you blessings—joy, peace, and contentment—when you serve Him by doing what He desires for you to do.

Joy

Happiness and joy are so connected in our minds that it is often hard to separate the two. The Bible never commands us to be happy.

As Solomon learned, chasing happy is a fruitless pursuit. But doing what God designed for us to do produces joy—an inward assurance that God has everything under control.

As Paul illustrated in Philippians, joy is deeper than pain, stronger than suffering, and greater than grief. It springs from pursuing what is eternal rather than chasing what is temporary.

Joy is one of God's gifts when you magnify Him and fulfill the purpose that He has for you. He gives it to you because joy is contagious, and it's the best proof that Christianity is real. As A.W. Tozer said, "A company of pure-living and cheerful Christians in the community is a stronger proof that Christ is risen than any learned treatise."[1]

Peace

Often, when we hear the word *peace*, we think of two countries ceasing to be at war. But the Bible speaks of an internal peace that every believer can have. When you trust Christ, you immediately experience peace with God. The sins that separate you from God are forgiven because of Christ's sacrifice on the cross.

Paul called the peace of God something "which surpasses all understanding" (Philippians 4:7). That is, it is impossible to comprehend with our natural minds. But understand it or not, the peace of God is possible because Jesus lives in your heart. When Isaiah prophesied that Christ would come, he called Jesus the Prince of Peace. And when Jesus was sharing with His disciples about the difficulties they could face after He ascended to heaven, He said, "I have said these things to you, that in me you may have peace. In the world you will have tribulation. But take heart; I have overcome the world" (John 16:33).

Contentment

Joy is the presence of a positive emotion. Peace is the absence of a negative one, such as anxiety. Together, joy and peace produce contentment.

Solomon proved that if a person has everything they want, they discover everything is not enough. Discontentment is trying to fill a void with stuff. And when we lack contentment, we fall for quick ways to fill the hole in our hearts. For example, we will go into extensive debt to buy more things.

The contentment our Heavenly Father gives as a reward for pursuing His purpose isn't complacency. It is not an excuse for lack of motivation. No, the contentment God puts in your heart is a freedom from greed and envy. It is gratitude for what you have instead of frustration from what you don't.

Joy, peace, and contentment were what Solomon and every person in history wanted. They can be yours when your mission is to glorify God and your purpose is His purpose for your life.

Everyday Habits

After you determine that you want to live your purpose, the logical question that follows is how to do it. You want help finding your purpose and a road map to put your plans into action.

Paul gave instructions for finding and fulfilling your purpose in the final chapter of Philippians. His instructions are simple. The secret is to practice them every day.

Rejoice in the Lord

Every morning and throughout the day, Paul said believers should "rejoice in the Lord." And to emphasize his point, he repeated it again more emphatically, "Again I will say, rejoice" (Philippians 4:4).

Rejoicing isn't forcing yourself to act like you are happy when life isn't going well. Rejoicing isn't shouting "Praise the Lord!" when your house burns, your parent dies, or you are involved in an accident. Rejoicing in the Lord is choosing to focus on the eternal plan of God, how your Heavenly Father will turn your pain or grief into something productive. It is allowing the Holy Spirit, amid your tears, to comfort you when you are hurting. And it is remembering to express your gratitude when things are going well and when you are blessed with good things.

The best way to rejoice in the Lord is to start your day spending time with Him and memorizing a Bible verse—a verse you can meditate on during the day. Rejoicing in the Lord is staying focused on the goodness of God.

Serve Others

When I started in ministry, I was young and inexperienced. My preaching wasn't very effective, nor was it spiritually deep. And, like all young preachers, I wanted to speak in large churches and before large crowds.

Those opportunities didn't come. Instead, I was invited to nursing homes and small group Bible studies. At first, I felt these invitations were a waste of my time. Often, in a nursing home, the elderly residents fell asleep or didn't comprehend what I was saying.

I was discouraged, of course, but something happened in my heart. I discovered serving was better than preaching. Those elderly residents just wanted someone to talk to them, to listen to their stories, or laugh at their jokes.

I found that ministry is service. Once I made serving others my priority, God began to develop the ministry I have today. God, in His goodness, has allowed me to speak before large crowds and in large churches. But the thrill is still in serving.

When Paul paused in his letter to address the personal conflict between Euodia and Syntyche, he told the other believers to help them work out their differences. And when Paul spoke of Timothy and Epaphroditus, he commended their service to him and the churches. Service is the first result of rejoicing in the Lord and the first step to finding your purpose.

Pray

So many have heard so much about prayer but practice it so little. Prayer is as important as turning on the light when you enter a dark room. Without prayer, you won't be able to find your way.

But prayer is essential if you are going to fulfill your purpose. You will need the strength and guidance that only come through praying. Paul expressed the need in Philippians 4:6, saying, "Do not be anxious about anything, but in everything by prayer and supplication with thanksgiving let your requests be made known to God."

The instruction to pray has three distinct words: *prayer, supplication,* and *thanksgiving.* Prayer describes an act of worship where you spend time intentionally praising and adoring God for who He is. Prayer can include quoting verses in the Bible about God to God. He loves the adoration from your lips. And praising His character builds your faith in Him.

Supplication is sharing your requests with God. It isn't telling God what to do, but sharing what your heart desires Him to do. God already knows your heart and your desires, but James stated that "you do not have, because you do not ask [God]" (James 4:2).

Finally, time spent with your Heavenly Father should include a time of thanksgiving. Praise is expressing who God is, but thanksgiving is expressing gratitude for what the Lord has done for you. Our Lord loves a grateful heart. But it is easy for us to assume God knows we are thankful, so we never take the time to simply tell Him, "Thank You."

Leprosy was a horrible disease when Jesus walked on earth. It disfigured individuals and made them social outcasts. Most lepers became beggars. Jesus once encountered ten lepers who pleaded for mercy and healing. Jesus told them to show themselves to the priests so they could be restored to society. It was another way of saying their wish was granted and they were healed.

But of the ten lepers who got what they wanted, only one returned to thank Jesus. When you are praying, don't be like the nine ungrateful lepers. Be like the one who told God "Thank You" for His blessings.

*Prayer is as important as turning on
the light when you enter a dark room.*

Think Good Thoughts

In recent years, medical science has found the effects our thoughts have on our lives. Thoughts affect our emotions, our actions, and our health.

But long before scientists discovered the power of thoughts, Paul understood the effects. Good thoughts and godly thoughts are vital to a life filled with joy, peace, and contentment. Paul knew that you have more control over your thoughts than you imagine. That is why he listed thoughts to occupy your mind in Philippians 4:8:

- Godly thoughts dwell on what is true. Worry thinks about untruths and rumors.

- Godly thoughts dwell on what is honest and honorable, especially about yourself. Negative thoughts repeat lies about your sins and who you are in Christ.

- Godly thoughts dwell on what is just. Anger thinks only of revenge.

- Godly thoughts dwell on purity. Lust dwells on impure thoughts and ideas.

- Godly thoughts dwell on what is lovely. Anxiety sees the "what-ifs" in every situation.

- Godly thoughts dwell on the commendable and good
  in others. Jealousy thinks only of getting its way and
  repeating gossip.

The last two things Paul mentioned relate to thoughts that turn your heart to praising God. When you see things that have excellence, you see your blessings. When you think of things that are worthy of praise, you express it to your Heavenly Father.

It is a slogan often quoted, and it is true: You aren't what you think you are, but what you think, you are. So, while pursuing your purpose, think godly thoughts.

Give and Receive

Generosity is a characteristic of every person living the assignment God has for them in His plan. Generosity means I share my time and the wisdom I've gained by studying the Bible. It is sharing words of encouragement and giving my material possessions to others.

Paul was a giver. Literally, he gave everything for the cause of Christ.

Paul was also a receiver. The apostle thanked the Philippians for sending money to pay for some of his expenses. In fact, the church at Philippi was the only church that supported Paul when he started.

The purpose our Heavenly Father has for you may involve a need for money to fulfill it. You, of course, must be willing to give from your resources if you expect others to give. But when others give to help you, you must be a gracious receiver.

Early in my ministry, people often tried to give me financial gifts but, most of the time, I refused to accept them.

One day, an elderly lady handed me a $20 bill. She knew I was planning a mission trip and said she wanted to help pay my airfare. I knew she probably needed the money more than I did. I politely declined to take it. To my surprise, she scolded me. She said, "Sir, you are full of pride."

Shocked by her words, I replied, "I don't understand why you said that."

She looked me in the eye and said, "Because you won't receive what the Lord told me to give you. And the reason you won't take it is because you want to tell people you did it on your own." Then she paused, put the money back into my hand, and continued. "Now, take this. I'm not going to let you rob me of the blessing of participating in your ministry."

I knew how to give, but I had to learn how to receive.

Sometimes, the gift isn't money. It might be a compliment or a recommendation. It may be the gift of advice when you seek counsel. But when you are doing what God wants you to do, be sure to give and to receive.

Trust God

Throughout the Bible, when God revealed His purpose for someone's life, the revelation was followed by a crisis of faith:

- When God told Noah to build the ark, the people mocked him. He had to trust God.

- When God told Abraham to sacrifice his son, Abraham had to take a leap of faith and trust that God knew what He was doing.

- When God told Moses to lead the children of Israel out of Egypt, Moses immediately told God that he lacked the ability to confront Pharaoh and suggested He ask someone else. But God *had* equipped Moses, and God's response was for Moses to trust Him.

- When the Lord told the Israelites to march around Jericho, the people were confused. This battle plan didn't make any sense. They had to trust God.

- When God told Gideon to take 300 men into battle against a larger army, the odds were against him. He had to trust God.

- When Gabriel told Mary that she was pregnant with the Messiah, she had to trust God.

- Throughout Jesus's ministry, He told people to take up their bed and walk, to step out of the boat, and to stretch forth their hands. In addition, the disciples had to leave their occupations and follow Jesus. All involved trust.

- Peter, Paul, and all the leaders of the early church had to trust God, even when persecution meant losing everything.

Living your purpose involves faith in the One who made you and called you to your purpose. Trust Him.

A Final Charge

If you are like most people, there is one question in your mind: *What is my purpose?* More than anything, you would like for me or someone to answer that question.

But I can't. And here is why: I don't know what motivates you, what you're passionate about, or what gives you satisfaction when you do it. I don't know your abilities or what you do well. I don't know your personality or your people skills. If I were forming a choir, I wouldn't know what part you should sing or where you should stand. I wouldn't even be able to tell you if you should be in the choir.

But I know Someone who knows all these things about you and more. He is your Heavenly Father, the God of the universe. He designed you before you were born, determined how He would use you to accomplish His plan, and then gifted you with the skills necessary to do it. And He put you in the right place surrounded by the right people.

So, why don't you ask Him what your role is? Trust me, He will show you. He showed me, and He has shown others. And He will show you.

Paul's final words to the Philippians contained two statements that demonstrate what happens when you trust God with your purpose. The first statement teaches that you have all the strength you need. The second one shows you have all the resources available to do it.

Nothing Is Impossible

Paul's first affirmation is in Philippians 4:13. He writes, "I can do all things through him who strengthens me."

Motivational speakers often tell people they have the ability within themselves to achieve anything. Sadly, the listeners learn very quickly they don't. Paul, on the other hand, didn't suggest that people fulfilling their purpose in life are superhumans. Instead, they are humans with supernatural strength—a strength that comes from a supernatural God. And Paul knew God was powerful enough to get him out of prison or to give him strength to endure prison.

And it is the same power that enables you to accomplish your purpose. In your spiritual walk, whatever you need, whenever you need it, and wherever you need it, that supernatural power is always available.

Endless Supply

The second affirmation Paul gave is in Philippians 4:19: "My God will supply every need of yours according to his riches in glory in Christ Jesus."

Your purpose will present needs. In Christ, they will be met. Need patience? He will supply all the patience you need. Need wisdom? Guidance? You have a Bible that gives you the insight you need. Discernment? Opportunities? Support? These are available in unlimited supply, and the Holy Spirit will guide you every step of the way.

God's provision may not come as quickly as you wish or in the way you desire. But it will come.

Your purpose will present needs.
In Christ, they will be met.

Chasing Joy

I stepped onto the plane and settled into my seat. The frequent flier miles came in handy, getting me upgraded to first class. The flight attendant brought me a diet soda. I took a moment to catch my breath since I'd had to rush to make my connection.

Once I am settled, I normally start reading the latest historical biography that I purchased. But today was different. Instead of reading, I sat in my seat watching people as they boarded the plane. A sweet young couple with two preschoolers walked by. Then came a businessman dressed in a suit that had seen better days. A teenager listening to music, oblivious to those around him, passed me too.

Then she appeared. A preppy young lady entered the plane. She sat down across the aisle from me. I noticed as she leaned her head back that she had been crying.

My mind immediately flashed back to Jenna, the young lady I met several years ago on a similar flight. I have often wondered what happened to her. I remember seeing a news anchor in Oklahoma City one night on the television that resembled her. If it was her, she was using a different name from the one I remember.

Maybe she found her Prince Charming, is the mother of two wonderful kids, and is having a good life. But I am curious if she found the happiness that she desperately wanted. Not if she kept seeking it the same way as she was when we met.

And I wonder about Randy, the wrestler. I see him occasionally on a wrestling show. His age is starting to catch up with him. He isn't as quick or as strong as he was when we met. And based on his comments in interviews, I think he is still chasing happy, thinking one more car, one more dollar, and one more house will help him catch it.

But it won't. Never has. Never will.

Only Jesus and living the life He designed for you will bring you what you so desperately desire.

NOTES

1. A.W. Tozer, "The Truth's Most Powerful Ally," *The Set of the Sail* (Chicago, IL: Moody Publishers, 2018).

ABOUT THE AUTHOR

PHIL WALDREP is the founder and CEO of Phil Waldrep Ministries and host of Women of Joy, Gridiron Men, and Celebrators conferences—building up leaders and equipping nearly 60,000 annual attendees in the knowledge and love of Christ. He speaks regularly at churches and conferences across the United States.

OVERCOME PAST HURTS + BEGIN TO
TRUST AGAIN

BEYOND

BETRAYAL

PHIL WALDREP

FOREWORD BY ANN VOSKAMP
NEW YORK TIMES BESTSELLING AUTHOR

Whether you've been hurt by a family member, friend, colleague, or trusted leader, you are not alone. Even Jesus was betrayed. *Beyond Betrayal* offers biblical principles and practical tools that can help you identify your betrayers, avoid resentment, and choose forgiveness to move past your pain.

To learn more about Harvest House books and
to read sample chapters, visit our website:

www.harvesthousepublishers.com

HARVEST HOUSE PUBLISHERS
EUGENE, OREGON